God's Kingdom News

*Read the Good News
"Since the Beginning of Time"*

Articles from God

Transcribed by Janie Allen
Paintings by Dianne Guthrie

God's Kingdom News
© 2015 All rights reserved
Dianne Guthrie

ALL RIGHTS RESERVED. No part of this book may be reproduced in any form or by any means whatsoever, including photography, xerography, broadcast, transmission, translation into any language, or recording, without written permission in writing from the publisher. Reviewers may quote brief passages in critical articles or reviews.

Published by
Dianne Guthrie

CONTACT:
dianne.guthrie@hotmail.com

Cover art by Dianne Guthrie

Printed in the U.S.A.

Acknowledgements

Janie Allen's dear friend, Jane Turner, created early manuscripts of *The Kingdom News*.

These were distributed while both Janie and Jane were still with us. Their deaths occurred within days of each other - making them "sisters" in Christ here on earth, as well as in heaven.

Janie's husband, Dr. Don Allen, faithfully edited these early manuscripts.

Michael Gray developed the final version of *God's Kingdom News* by reviewing the early manuscripts and comparing them with Janie's original written and audio versions.

Janie's daughter, Dianne Guthrie, edited this transcription.

Dianne also painted the paintings that have been added to the book.

I want to personally thank each one of you this side of heaven and beyond for making God's message to us in *God's Kingdom News* "come to life."

—Dianne Guthrie

Contents

Introduction	1
God's Kingdom News	2
Life Breathed into a Newspaper	3
Free Will! Free Will!	5
Divinity	7
Wake Up Call!	9
Unity	10
Prophesy	11
The Day of the Lord	12
The End Time	13
The Church	15
Seasons	17
Glory!	19
Intercession	21
My Special Birthday Card	23
Persecution Comes	26
Holiness	27
Pride	28
Forgiveness and Repentance	29
Communion - The Lord's Supper	32
For The Children	34
Conversion	38

Year 2000	40
Discernment	41
Sleep	42
Healing	43
Light	44
Sacrifice	46
Mercy	48
Possessions	51
Predestination	52
Jerusalem, My Namesake	54
Divine Order	55
Thy Kingdom Come	56
Mother Mary	57
Love of God	63
Divine Conception	65
The Jew	66
Peace	68
The Hurting Church	69
Man	72
Soul Sleep	74
Provisions	76
Guilt	77
Song	79
Death	80

Precious Metals	82
Reprieve and Repentance	83
Look Up (Redemption)	84
The Crucifixion	85
Attitude Equals the Beatitude	87
Resurrection Day	88
Knowing God	90
Marriage: Human and Divine	92
Midnight Call	94
The Brain	96
Glory	97
Baptisms	99
Salvation	101
War Cry ("War" then "Peace") Part One	103
War Cry ("War" then "Peace") Part Two	105
My Passion	107
Truth (What is Truth?)	110
Identity (The Unity of the Human and Divine)	111
Light	113
Predestination	114
Wonder	115
Behold	117
Adolescence	121
Hope and Peace	122

Vanity (Vain) 123

The Kingdom of God. 124

Coming Again 125

Our Father (Father's Day) Part One 126

Our Father (Father's Day) Part Two 127

War & Peace 128

The Brain (Computer and Human) 129

What Is Truth? 131

Life, Death, Resurrection 133

Fear 135

Resolve and Resolutions: Mine and Yours. 137

Janie Allen

Introduction

Janie Allen, daughter of God, faithfully sought and listened for God's voice.

She transcribed what she heard and recorded each message for future generations to hear and follow.

Janie was a delightful, engaging woman who never met a stranger. No one who came across her path left without feeling the love of Jesus and hearing about His Salvation Plan. Many souls have been won to Christ through her ministry. She was "irresistible" for Christ's sake.

Kingdom News is God's newspaper. As Janie wrote… It all started one day when I was reading secular newspapers such as the Jerusalem Post and other magazines. Suddenly the Lord said, "Would you like to know what I have in mine? I have a newspaper; and it's called *The Kingdom News*."

The following pages are the result of this conversation.

Janie loved to sing and remembered the old hymns in her own words and way.

Her versions are included throughout these pages.

—Dianne Guthrie (Janie Allen's daughter)

God's Kingdom News
by God

To My beloved daughter, Janie - Why has it been this long before we have had a conversation of this nature? I have given you this unique gift to be used, not to be wasted on other things that take up your time. Yes, I desire to use your hand each day for our diary, yours and mine. Much wealth in the spiritual realm is taking place on My time clock. I want you in on My Kingdom News. Today's news: The wicked are becoming more wicked. The Saints are becoming more Holy and Saintly. The blind are becoming more blinded. The seers are seeing more clearly. Hell is moving closer to earth. Heaven is ready to merge with earth. Those are My headlines...

Life Breathed into a Newspaper
by Janie Allen

It all started one day when I was reading secular newspapers such as the Jerusalem Post and other magazines. Suddenly, the Lord said, "Would you like to know what I have in Mine? I have a newspaper; and it's called The Kingdom News. Would you like to know what the news is and what My headlines are?" He just interrupted me and gave me those words. I thought, "Well, that's different." Of course, I said, "Yes, I would, Lord." And so, now and then, nearly every week, I will go to the Lord and get the *Kingdom News* headlines and stories. Here they are.

"But I (God) can and will deliver those imprisoned…"

Free Will! Free Will!
by God

Free will - free choices. Do My children choose life or death? That is their choice - life in Me or death in the other kingdom. This one gift of Mine is the most important gift for all mankind - life in the Vine. The alternative is death in the pit. Every day in your earthly life these choices have to be made. It is a day-by-day decision. In Me, one always has that choice. In Satan, once captured by him, free will is destroyed. You are imprisoned, bound, and eventually destroyed. His enticements are enjoyable for a while but soon become enslavement. But I (God) can and will deliver those imprisoned if they turn to Me with all their heart, soul, body, and mind, and receive My Power (the Holy Spirit) to turn around and go another direction completely.

Repentance is the name of that direction. Much prayer is needed for these souls to be delivered before and afterwards. Satan is a roaring lion always ready to pounce on My people. But My Hand is not shortened. It is always ready to save, heal, and deliver. My Love for you is overwhelming. My Power toward you is without measure. How can you resist Me? I desire for you to walk with Me and talk with Me and let Me tell you, you are My own. My Love is everlasting.

A song - "And He walks with me, and He talks with me. And He tells me I am His own."

His is of the flesh, in the soulish realm. Mine is in the spiritual realm (Agape Love). It is a choice. Life in Me or death in him. Oh, My children, how I want to gather you up in My arms. Your Abba Father.

Prayer from Janie Allen - That you can feel the Love of God. I ask the Lord to anoint these lines, this message, so that you can feel His Love coming through. How He wants to gather you up and hug all of you into His arms, to cover you, just cover you completely with His Love.

Amen.

"Only Your Father in Heaven can give you the breath of life and breathe on you the ingredient of divinity…"

DIVINITY
by God

Divinity equals divine grace (infinite grace). I AM divine. Only with My Spirit of Grace can you be too. Divinity is eternity. Only your Father in Heaven can give you the breath of life and breathe on you the ingredient of divinity, which is My Spirit of Grace. Now stop, My little one, and breathe in My Spirit of Grace to make you into My sons and daughters.

Can you fathom such a God as you have? I AM not really just a God, but an essence, your Father, your Creator, even your Daddy! I desire an intimate relationship with mankind. I did not create you and then leave you fatherless like My creation is doing today.

I created you and gave you My Divinity, even to make it possible for you to become priests and kings. Why have so few of you attained this? Jesus Christ, the Messiah, Anointed One, is Your Heavenly King. And David, son of Jesse, is your earthly king. But now, I AM looking for priests and kings in My Kingdom of God (My Church). There is a way - it is Trust and Obey.

Here is a song, "Trust and obey, for there's no other way, to be happy in Jesus but to trust and obey."

You say that sounds so easy. No, it is not. The road is wide; but the gate is narrow. But with your Father God, all things are possible. Oh My children, My sons and daughters, your Heavenly Father did not leave you fatherless. My ear is always open to your call. My Hand is not shortened that it cannot save and heal all who come to Me with a repentant and open heart. My Son, Jesus Christ, is at the door ready for you to turn the knob. Oh, how We want you to open that door. Selah!

"...repent and look up..."

WAKE UP CALL!
by God

Church...Wake up! Do you not see? Do you not hear? Do you not know that the world is being terminated all around you in every direction? Sin is personified. Devastation is everywhere; and my people sleep on and on and on. My prophets' voices are not heard on planet earth. How much longer will I cry out through them to repent and look up; that your redemption is running out?

Grace is coming to a close. Free will no longer will be. You will be left holding on to your very lives unless you turn to Me with all your heart and souls and have no other gods before Me. My child, can you not hear your Father's cry, crying loudly for His children to leave their possessions behind and come and follow Me and reach up higher on that ladder to My Abode? My Heart is pounding and bleeding out for My Creation. We want all of you with Us, forever and ever. We desire that none perish. How can you resist your Father's wish?

My Love for you is everlasting. Can you not feel My distress for and over you this very day? I have protected you and guarded you all your days, but night is coming and you need Me and more and more of My Spirit to pull you through. Please let Him pour His oil in your lamp or vessels. He wants to wet your wicks and light your life with His light and bring you home to your bridegroom without spot or blemish. Please! Please! Please! Don't push Him away. Let Him embrace you with My love - Divine Love for your Divinity. Hold fast, hold on and be My Bride that overcomes! Your Trinity.

UNITY
by God

Unity, my little one, is the provision for My Spirit to permeate your groups, family, church, Bible classes, friendships, and even the Nations. Even in the other kingdoms (secular), this law holds forth. Remember the Tower of Babel? They were in one accord.

The Christian church is most attacked by the spirit of disunity, disharmony, and dissension. These things are brought about by lies, gossip, and false prophets. Even My choice ones can be deceived.

Lord, how do we keep this from happening?

Love (unconditional) and humility are your best weapons. Also, be kind to one another. As your Father in Heaven has forgiven you, you are required to forgive. Forgiveness brings forth unity as no other trait. It is an act of the will. Do you choose not to forgive and be separated from Me and them? If you choose to forgive, I will give you favor with Me and them.

Only when the prayer in John 17 comes to pass will you be one, and the world will be won. Love one another as I have loved you; then My Spirit will bring forth unity; and all will be one. Your not obeying this one word is holding back your King from His imminent return. Selah.

Stop and think on this. With Me, all things are possible. Your Loving Father, Your God.

Prophesy
by God

Thus sayeth the Word of God. My words are alive and health and healing to all your bones, sinews, and tissues. The Word of God is quick and powerful and sharper than any two-edged sword, pressing even into the innermost parts of your body and quickening even your spirit and soul. How much more do you need? Jesus is the proclamation of My words and flesh. Did He not say, "Even so send I you, as the living Father sent Me?"

He would not send you without all the provisions needed by My Spirit which is the action of the Godhead? He is our workhorse. Ride with Him; and you will win your race. You will not come in second or third, but first place. You will overcome and be My glorious church, without spot or blemish.

How do you like these words? Do you not know you have many cheerleaders cheering you on?

They are the body of all the believers that have gone before you.

When you win the race of your day-by-day battles, their faces are all aglow and they jump for joy. Just picture how a warrior in the worldly race responds.

Beloved, you are never alone in My realm. Only do you feel loneliness in the natural realm, especially the worldly realm. Like the song says, "Count your blessings... name them one by one. Count your many blessings. See what God has done for his children." How very special you are to Me. Only Jesus and the Holy Spirit knows. This is why We always abide at your side and within your hide. This is Truth yesterday, today, and forever.

Your Abba Father.

THE DAY OF THE LORD
by God

Yes, My daughter, I have shown you many things that will happen and are already showing up. My Day of Rest, in the book of Hebrews, is soon to break forth. Many have misunderstood this day and thought it was possible to obtain now or in their lifetime. But it is for a future date. Now that day is about to unfold; and some of My saints will be ready to enter in. Make your vessels ready as Joshua did. He had no fear, doubt, or unbelief of My Power. My Fire did not burn them because My Love protected them by the cloud of My Holy Spirit (mist and rain). Are you ready to fight the battle of Jericho as Joshua did long ago? For there is a battle coming forth - the good fight of faith.

Song: "Soon and very soon, you are going to see the Lord. Soon and very soon, you are going to see the Lord." Hallelujah!

'And you will meet Him in the air. Declare! Declare! This is the day, this is the day that the Lord hath made. Let us rejoice and be glad in it. From your Father God to His children.

"Just look all around you at My Creation."

THE END TIME
by God

Rejoice, all My beloved children, those I have called and chosen to see My Glory and to be seers of My Revelations of things shortly to come to pass. Rejoice! Look up! Your redemption is nigh! I will come quickly. No time to look back. Remember Lot's wife? What a tragedy, for earthly things are nothing like heavenly things. Please My children, do not attach yourselves to this ground (earth) for it simply cannot compare to Holy Ground. I AM your Creator. I love beauty as you love beauty. Just look all around you at My Creation.

The elements, animals, seasons, snow, rain, ice - all things I have set before your eyes to behold My Beauty and glorify Me. Only when it goes amiss does it get reported. Your enemy is the destroyer and runs havoc with

My Creation from time to time.

Remember, I gave you power over all the powers of your enemy. I have said all this to say - your God loves you and has provided all things for you now and in the world to come, for you are My Inheritance. Just watch and see the splendor of it all. Wow! It's truly something to behold. How can I explain all this to you without My Holy Spirit to interpret and the precious blood of your Jesus, My Son, and His all-encompassing blood to cover all your sins now and forever? Receive Him and His suffering death on the cross for all mankind; and be My sons and daughters and His Bride, always at His side now and forever more. Does this make you happy, My children? Selah

Song, "This is the day, this is the day, that the Lord has made, that the Lord has made."

This is the beginning of the seventh day of creation. (Genesis 1 and 2) You are at 12:00 midnight of the sixth day - man's day.

Your Alpha and Omega God - Omnipotent, Omnipresent, and All-Powerful.

"...My church will be in order too, by and by."

THE CHURCH
by God

My Church. My People. My Kingdom. My Body. My City. My Dominion. My World. That is what My Church is to Me. It is the Kingdom of God on earth. My will be done. My Kingdom come on earth as it is in Heaven. That will be the end of My desire for My earthly church. My Body (the Church) is made up of individual souls or cells like in the human body. Each one is a living component of the whole body - My Body of which I AM the Head and you, as a whole, are My Heart. I AM in tune to every beat of your pulse. When one component of your body is out of order or broken or amiss, your body cannot function properly. All has to be in tune for unity of bodily parts to function properly. My Body is likened and similar to yours, to your own. Each organ has to be in place and in tune to its director, Me, your Head - Jesus Christ. Your body has to be in tune to the Holy Spirit to function correctly. He is the Captain of your body and the Captain of My Church. I AM the Head; and He is the Captain or Director of My Church. This is somewhat complicated; but I believe you can understand. Our Heavenly Father and Creator has planned it all from the beginning of time. All creation is divinely created to function in order. Even your earthly body and My Church will be in order too, by and by.

The Body now is coming together through persecutions and trials and fire. Soon too, Body and Head will function in one complete unit. The future church, iglesia, will prevail; and hell cannot cast it down. Your Savior and Lord.

"The future church, iglesia, will prevail..."

SEASONS
by God

(*This article relates to a struggling married couple.*)

To My beloved two. As you know, My loved ones, the victory is the Lord's. Now rest in Me. A heavenly army is at your rescue. Stand! Stand! The battle is the Lord's.

My Hand is not shortened that it cannot save and heal your whole family. Please release your faith and your love toward Me and them and watch their salvation come forth. Death always comes before life. Look at the seasons. Spring comes after winter. All of My own will die in some way before I come for them. All flesh will vanish; and only Spirit will remain. I know you are only made of dust and have been brought forth by My Holy Spirit. But still, you are not glorified and cannot see the future.

The faith walk is what I AM requiring of all of My church now and until I come. Life in Me or death by him, your enemy, is a daily choice. My Hand is on you to carry you through this dark tunnel into the beautiful sunset of your earthly life. My heart is overflowing with passionate love for you and yours.

I love your praises and songs for Me and to Me.

Your Abba Father

GLORY!

by God

Habakkuk and Isaiah 11. My Kingdom Come, My will be done that the knowledge of the Glory of the Lord will cover the earth as the waters cover the seas. Then I will have a people to call Me their God; and My Shekinah Glory will be on each one to reflect Me in them. This is your Father's Heart - to share His Glory with His Creation. Since Adam sinned and failed, My Glory has been hidden from mankind. Now there is a break in the Heavens; and My Glory is beginning to fall on My people like rain and snowflakes.

My Kingdom on earth is once again being penetrated by My Shekinah Glory. As My Spirit moves like the wind and you never know where or when, so shall My Glory come through. Many, many of you are discerning your Father's Will to share His Glory and have been under the Glory cloud. My only Son, Jesus Christ, has made all this possible. He is the first fruit; and My Saints are following His trail. My children, you can even smell My Glory on others. You can feel My Glory on yourselves. You can see the Glory all around you. Yes! It is weighty and can pull or knock you down. Look into My Word and see how many times this occurred in the Old and the New Testaments. My loved ones, just to be in your Father's Presence is glorious. Abide!

Abide! Abide!

Song - "Oh, the Glory of His Presence."

"My Glory is beginning to fall on My people..."

INTERCESSION
by God

Yes, My daughter, intercession is the strongest manner of prayer available for My Saints. If I have called you into intercession for My Glory, you are a chosen vessel to be made without spot or blemish. You have been quickened to render yourselves to the heart of your Father and Master. This is a life within a life that most of the body knows not of. Do you know all that takes place during your times of intercession?

One. Chains are broken on lives.
Two. Souls are able to feel My Love.
Three. Principalities are removed.
Four. Minds are released to hear My Voice.
Five. Free choices are given back to Saints and sinners.
Six. Cities can be taken back.
Seven. Nations can be overthrown.
Eight. Marriages can be mended.
Nine. Churches can be reconciled.
Ten. Peace can prevail.
Eleven. Souls can be prepared for salvation.

Twelve. I do not respond until My saintly intercessors are on their knees in prayer with moans and groans. Deep intercession brings forth powerful eruptions in My Kingdom. My friends, world without sin is the end. Intercession is your tool to bring forth your King and world without sin. My intercessors who respond to their calling will always sit at My side and abide. I AM the Vine, you are the branches. Without Me and the Holy Spirit, you are nothing and can do nothing. With Me, this world can be won. Oh, how important you are to Me.

"...*render yourselves to the heart of your Father and Master*..."

MY SPECIAL BIRTHDAY CARD
by Janie Allen

It was my birthday two days ago. I asked the Lord, for that day, would He give me a love letter for my birthday. And He did. But first, I will give some background on me.

I was born in 1924 with an incurable blood disease. It was an inherited disease that the doctors traced back to King George III, of all things, and was called porphyria. It is a demonic, horrible disease of mankind.

By 1971, I had been inside a house for four and a half years. I could not walk outside. I could not sit by a window; and I could not ride in a car. Hundreds of common "every day" chemicals would provoke the disease, bringing it forth. It was a killer disease. I was in the house waiting to die.

Later that year, I attended a Kathryn Kuhlman convention in Memphis, Tennessee at the Assembly of God Church on Highland. I had heard of the Holy Spirit; yet it was sort of a mystery. But the Holy Spirit did go through my body. It was pulling me to the floor in the Assembly of God Church. I didn't know what it was. It was a Power. It was a Force. It went on for about thirty or forty seconds. It was like a broken record that came through and told me I was cured! I was cured! I was cured! Now, I wouldn't have used that word, cured. I wasn't hurting or anything; but it was strange. So I held onto my chair and stopped it.

God miraculously touched me; and He healed me. The Holy Spirit went through my body. It was like in Ephesians when Paul asked the Ephesians if they had ever received the Holy Spirit since they believed. "Well," they said, "We've never even heard of the Holy Spirit. We were baptized with John's baptism." And mine was almost the same way. That was in 1971. It's my history; but it's His Story - that of Jesus and the power of the resurrection. So I know a little bit about that resurrection power. I know a lot more about it now, after these twenty-nine years.

Like I say, I live to tell His Story.

It was early morning on May 18th, about 5:00 a.m. I was awake. I don't usually wake up that early; but for some reason, I did that morning. It was my birthday; and I was probably excited about it. There's something special about your birthday. So I feel like the Lord is telling me this is for everyone. This letter is for you on your birthday. Here it goes.

I just said, "Jesus?"

And He said, "Yes?"

And I said, "Tell me you love me more than ever today because it's my birthday."

Jesus said, "I love you, My little one, more than the universe contains. My love for you is everlasting, a world without end. My love for you is like a hot coal, burning in an incendiary. Can you fathom that? My love for you is like a thousand birds singing all at once. I have formed you and ordained you to be a life giver to Me and others. Your love sustains Me for others. Because I live, are your tomorrows. Fear not, My child. Your future I hold. Wisdom, with Love, is your fate. My birthday wish for you is this. Fear no evil. Speak no evil. See no evil. Think no evil. Do no evil. Happy Birthday, My adoring bride. Abide. Abide. Abide."

The birthday card came out which I thought was most unusual (especially the end). But whatever He gives to me is profound. It's not only for me. I feel like it was for everyone on their birthday. Also, a lot of times it comes out with a song afterwards. These are the songs that came out after that birthday message.

I know I can't sing; but the Holy Spirit, for some reason, does like to sing through me. So I'm going to just let Him do it.

> "Love makes the world go round. Love makes the world go round. God sent His Son to you He won. Love makes the world go round."

I love that song. It was written a long time ago, but I still love it. And another verse came out.

These were His verses, not mine.

> "Faith makes the world go round. Faith makes the world go round. I can move mountains, yours and Mine, when faith comes around."

And the next verse was,

> *"Grace makes the world go round; Grace makes the world go round. My Love for you fulfills all love. Grace makes the world go round."*

And the next one is a song that comes through me so many times. I don't know why; but this song does.

> *"There is a river, the streams you know not of. There is a river flowing with My Love. Come to the waters and bathe from streams above. Come to the waters and be immersed with My Love."*

It ends, "Your Agape Father and Holy Spirit". And a lot of hearts came out. One, two, three, four, five, six, seven, eight, nine, ten hearts — and I drew the pictures of the heart.

He said, "This is your birthday card from the Trinity.

Because, as I said before, it was 5:00 a.m. in the morning when I got all that. I was just ready to ascend. I closed my eyes; and all this started coming out again. I thought, this is just too good to not continue to write on. So I turned the light back on and got my pen. And this is what continued to flow.

> *"My love for you is like Niagara Falls, pouring down on you with streams of love.*
>
> *My love for you is like the sun, beaming down on you with rays of love.*
>
> *My love for you is like snowflakes, with each flake melting on your face.*
>
> *My love for you is like the rain, flooding your soul with My sweet refrain.*
>
> *My love for you is like sugar, each grain is sweet as perfume on your lips."*

His love is beyond description. You cannot describe the love that God has for His children. You cannot describe it. The only thing that I can tell you is to feel it. And I'm asking you now just to let His love from above come down and touch you and immerse you and caress you. There's no feeling like it. You cannot contain it. All you want to do is give it out to others. And that is what he wants you to do. Pass it on.

Persecution Comes
by God

The year 1999 is soon to end. My Judgments came and went. Many lives were destroyed. Some of My Saints were removed from you. Other lives were spared to choose once again, life in Me or destruction in the destroyer. I love you, My people. My Hand is always there to pull you up and out of your fires of destruction if you will only turn to Me and repent. I AM the Key and the Way to Life in eternity. Repent! Repent now, My loved ones, before it is too late. My judgments have been coming. (The book of Daniel is being fulfilled now before your very eyes.)

Yes, many of My Saints are being martyred and persecuted for their faith; and many more of you will be until I come. Persecution has come and is coming to My precious Saints. Those of you who know Me and are involved in souls and do not love your lives unto death (Revelation), will receive My White Stone of commitment.

My Heavenly Saints are standing and applauding you, even now, and cheering you on. And remember you are never alone for I, the Father, and Jesus, My Son and your Savior are with you and inside of you. Flesh and blood will not inherit the Kingdom of Heaven - only My Spirit ones. So don't ever be afraid of the evil one who can only destroy flesh and soul. I AM-My Word (the Bible) is the deciding factor. Heaven and earth will pass; but My Words will remain. I leave you with this (in capital letters), FEAR NOT! I have overcome this world. And you will too because I AM in you and we are in our Father. Remember, you are My passion.

PASSION.

HOLINESS
by God

Be ye holy. Why? Because I AM Holy. I in you and you in Us can equal Holiness. From the beginning of time, this was Our plan. We are family. I AM your Father; and you are My children. Mother earth is not your mother as some are now believing.

"Father, who is?" (Mary Jane Allen)

My True Church birthed you by My Holy Spirit. I AM your Father and Maker. Read Genesis 1. We breathed the breath of Life in you; and you became a living body, soul, and spirit. Then, in Adam, all died. But then again, in Jesus Christ, all are made alive. I made you holy once again. Do you choose to remain; or do you choose to vacillate back and forth? It is a daily choice. Do you choose life or death? To live is for Christ; and death is gain. Be like Paul. Die daily so We can live in and through you; and you will be holy.

Pride
by God

Yes, today's headline and spotlight is on pride, your worst enemy. Everyone has it to a degree and some too much and some too little. There is a misconception about this word. There is false pride. That is where the Christian is in error. Teachers, ministers, and people of the cloth easily fall into this pit. They are tempted as none others. That is why, in My Word, I have concentrated on this subject continuously. This one sin opens you up to so many others and destroys My Work in you and for you. That is why you go through so many trials and fires and get burned so many times. Pride (false) always comes before a great fall. I AM the Vine; and you are the branches. Without Me, you can do nothing. Remember your beginning, only dust. I AM the Potter; and you are the clay.

Forgiveness and Repentance
by God

"Lord, please forgive me. I have put other things before Your time (our time). Lord, I love You and want to please You. Today, I give You my will to do Your will in and through me once again." (Mary Jane Allen)

You are forgiven, as I told you to forgive seventy times seven. You are forgiven every time you come to Me with a repentant heart as a child asking Me to forgive you. We are family. We will never, never turn our backs on you. We are Blood related. I AM your Father. Jesus is your Brother, Savior, Shepherd, Priest, King and soon will be your Kingdom Husband; now your Bridegroom-elect!

Now Our Holy Spirit is dressing you for that occasion. This is the most important and wonderful event ever to come to pass. Our Holy Spirit is your Groomsman. He is ever-present to dress and redress you in all your affairs and attire. Please don't push Him away. He is such a gentleman and very sensitive. He wants to meet your every need. He is oh, so gentle. Listen to His sweet and gentle nudging.

Howbeit, when He (the Spirit of Truth) comes, He will guide you into all Truth. He will not speak of Himself; but He will glorify Me (Jesus) and show you things to come.

"Thank you, thank you, again and again, Lord. I could not live without this strength from your well." (Mary Jane Allen)

"Jesus...now your Bridegroom-elect!"

"Listen to His sweet and gentle nudging."

Communion - The Lord's Supper
by God

As I have said in My Word, do this until I come, in remembrance of Me. You say, "How often?"

I say, "As often as I AM remembered."

My children, this is the crux of your salvation and living with Me here and in eternity. You are finite; and I AM infinite. You cannot grasp the meaning of all of this. But! Your enemy can and does accordingly. My Blood, your communion with Me, is your protection. Except you eat of My Flesh and drink of My Blood, there is no life in you. He will pass over you when He sees our communion. Remember the Blood on the door of the Israelites? I, your Savior, gave My life, body, and soul for this transformation. The soul is in the blood! (Leviticus 17:11).

Here is a song,

> *"Oh, how He loves you and me. He gave His Soul, His Life, His Blood, to make us whole. Oh, how He loves you and me."*

Here's another song,

> *"This is my story. This is my song. My Blood is your Savior, all your day long."*

Will you open your heart's door and let Me come in and sup with you?

Our Trinity and Divinity, yours and Mine.

"I, your Savior, gave My life, body, and soul for this transformation."

FOR THE CHILDREN
by God

My Children. My Creation. You are all children to Me. My Voice is heard mightily among My smaller children. They have no inhibitions. Preconceived ideas have not been established. So just tell them the simple truths of My Love and provisions for each of them. Tell them I have them in the palm of My Hand; and none such can pluck them out. Tell them to talk to Me; and I will listen and always answer. Tell them to pray for their earthly fathers and mothers and their friends and animals, too. All My creation will be in Heaven. Am I not a Creator of all things?

Tell them to fear not for their future; for I will guide their every step. Each one there today is so precious in My Sight. I know their name and every hair on their head. Tell them all they have to do is hold My Hand and listen to My Voice and ask Me; and I will guide them and protect them in all their activities.

My name is Jesus, their Savior. I shed My Blood for them and their protection from all harm.

Just tell them to say My Name out loud; and My Angels will surround them and keep them from hidden dangers because I died and rose again and went to Our Father in Heaven. I have left you a Comforter, a Protector, a Partner, one who can be with you, and even inside of you if you wish. Just ask Me and I will give this One to you. His Name is the Holy Spirit. He is the same One I had on earth to guide and protect Me and tell Me all the things My Father and your Father wanted Me to know - all wisdom, all knowledge, all understanding, all truth. He will even tell you things to come. (Isaiah 11) I desire for all of you to know Him as I did. He is very gentle and kind and would never make you do anything wrong or anything that you didn't want to do.

Howbeit, when He the Spirit of Truth hath come, he will guide you into all Truth. He will show you things to come and will not speak of Himself but will glorify Jesus Christ. (John 16:13)

When My Holy Spirit is with you and in control, you will have peace and feel My love and will be gentle and

Janie Allen

"My Children...Tell them to talk to Me."

"Each one there today is so precious in My Sight."

kind to one another. Also, My dear ones, it is by My Holy Spirit that I did all these miracles; for He is the Power of the Trinity - the Father, the Son, and the Holy Spirit. You see, He does all the work for us. It was even His Power that raised Me from the tomb. It was His Holy Spirit power that raised Lazarus from the grave. He, the Holy Spirit, abided in Me; and I used this Power and said, "Lazarus, come forth." In My name, the Holy Spirit will come forth for you too, and for your protection and to glorify the Father.

Remember, I have not given you a spirit of fear but love, power, and a sound mind. It is Your Father's good pleasure to give you all He has for all you have - your mind, your will, and your emotions. He is the Potter; and you are His clay. Please give Him your will this very day. I came to earth so you could come to Heaven. My Blood is your passport. This is your Easter message.

A song, *"Let Jesus come into your heart. Let Jesus come into your heart."*

Another song, *"Oh, how He loves you and me. Oh, how He loves you and me."*

CONVERSION
by God

Conversion=explosion. Just to commune with Me, My family, is a dynamic experience. Life in the Vine is Divine.

Conversion makes communion possible. This transaction is physical and spiritual - the most important in My whole universe. It is in no way man-made. It is an act of the Holy Spirit, the third Person of the Godhead. It was that act that brought Life into Mary's womb. It was that act that conceived you. It was that act that brought forth My whole universal church. It added a new dimension to your beings - new body, soul, and spirit. Before, it was just body and soul.

This is the mystery St. Paul speaks of. It is the crux of My Church. Without conversion, there is no church. This is a life-changing experience. How could one be the same with such an experience? Night becomes day. The Son (sun) begins to "shine you".

You are no longer blinded to spiritual happenings. You realize you have a Father in Heaven who loves you, gave His very Blood for you to bring you back to live with Him eternally. You are living in a brand new dimension. All things become new; old things are passed away. (1 Cor. 10:13)

> Born from the Spirit.
> Born from above.
> Born from the Spirit,
> Out of My Love.
> Now you have a new blood line.
> My Son gave you the transfusion.
> He was the Line

Janie Allen

That made you Divine.

You, My children, are My masterpiece, a whole new creation.

Stay in that vine. I AM the Vine.

Your Abba Father. His Name is the Holy Spirit.

Year 2000
by God

The year 2000 is upon you. My child, you know that a year in My calendar is but a day. Yes, I gave you the numerical number system. All things I have given you are for your and My use. This is just one way We can communicate. Satan also uses this form of communication. His ways are devious and demonic. Mine are always clear and to the point.

Back to My year of 2000. Are you disappointed that I did not show out or up? I was there all the time. Did you not remember in My Word that I AM coming when you and the world are not looking up or waiting for something to take place? I AM ready. Are you ready? My plans are still the same. I will not disclose any but to My prophets. You will know; for I will not do anything without letting you know.

My prophets today are watching and praying for My will to be revealed. Yes, My children, the time is very short now. Make yourselves ready for a departure. Set your table for Jesus, not Elijah. I AM so near and close to My people as never before. To some, it seems as if I have already come because We are one - one in the Spirit and one in the flesh. You know this is possible with all My Saints. The Kingdom of God can come upon you at any time. You know what I AM referring to. Now, be prepared. Look up, My Bride, your redemption is nigh; and your Bridegroom is at your side and ready for the ceremony by and by. My Holy Spirit is your groomsman dressing you in your wedding apparel, shiny and white, with glory all bright. I love My Bride without measure. To Me, you are oh so beautiful. Shine and reflect My Glory wherever you go.

DISCERNMENT
by God

This one gift I desire for all My children. Why don't all ask? It is yours for the asking.

Discernment is of the Spirit. My Holy Spirit is all-knowing and very discreet. Listen to His Voice. It is an inner Voice, an awareness of situations both good and evil. Many traps are set for you to fall into; but He, the Holy Spirit, has gone before you to guide your path. Hold His Hand at My command. He will unlock every door. Listen to His Voice and gentle nudging. He is a gentleman and will never make you surrender your will to His will. Because He is God, He knows all, sees all, and can do all. Because you are only one third spirit, you don't. He wants to share this gift with you. Just ask, believe, and receive. Discernment is of the Spirit. Much responsibility follows this gift.

Sleep
by God

What is it and why do we need it, you ask. Sleep is My way of restoring your body. Many scientists have also asked that question. In a way, it is a mystery to mankind. Death will follow if sleep is curtailed for any length of time. Sleep is a dimension that only your Maker, Father God, knows. It is a dimension also that your enemy can use to cause you to panic. Many battles of the mind are fought during sleep. Spirits, good and bad, can enter into My creation during sleep. Also, many problems can be solved during sleep.

Much, much healing is in process during sleep--healing of the mind, body, and spirit. In one sense, it is the process of life, death, and resurrection. It is also a procedure for your rehearsal of your death, burial, and resurrection into a new life dimension in My realm.

In your computer, sleep is more complicated than the state of being awake. Though your body is asleep, your mind and soul are not. They are transformed into another state of being and action. Men have not and will not unlock all My secrets of My creation. To them, sleep is the most questionable. I AM your Creator and know just what My creation needs to function properly. My earthly Creation needs sleep, water, air, food, light, and darkness and most of all, LOVE, to exist on planet earth. But even more, they need to know Me as their Father, Jesus as their Savior, and the Holy Spirit as their Paraclete. My little one, there is a lot here to ponder over.

Good night and sweet dreams.

I have and can reveal many divine revelations to My prophets and Saints during sleep periods. My Holy Spirit can and sometimes does pray through you during sleep. We have many dimensions to reach our Creation. Each function of your body is made for My pleasure; and worship can be done awake or asleep. Don't count sheep. Count your many blessings, name them one by one.

Here's a song, *"Count your many blessings, name them one by one. Count your many blessings; see what God has done. Count your blessings! Name them one by one. Count your many blessings; see what God has done."*

HEALING
by God

Say this verse, "Salvation is mine; healing is mine." Yes, I have given you this: salvation and healing through My Son's obedience, even to death on the cross. My Blood paved the way for your salvation and healing. Divine Blood for putrid blood! My Holy Spirit can purify your blood and give you a blood transfusion anytime you choose to commune with Me. You say, "Oh, really? That's hard to believe." I say, "With Me, all things are possible."

"You are My child; and I love you. I want you well and whole and provide this way for you to be. Your Father is willing. Are you willing to be made whole once again? Believe and receive." (Psalm 103)

I AM Jehovah, Your God.

Light

by God

Did I not say, in the beginning the world was null and void and absent of light? All was darkness. And then, did I not say, "Let there be light." And the light overtook the darkness.

Always, My child, My light will overtake your darkness. Now, as in the beginning, a great darkness is overtaking the world. The only light that will shine will be from My Saints who have abandoned themselves to Me to be made holy. The presence of My Holy Spirit will burn through them. My Glory will shine through their faces; and light will emanate from their presence.

Arise, shine, for thy light has come. Darkness will cover the earth; but brightness will explode through My people. Are you ready for this explosion? No, you are not. Remember the ten virgins? Some were ready; and some were not.

Now much oil is being poured into willing lamps (vessels). Soon, very soon, I, your God, will come and light these lamps (vessels). Many souls will run toward this light to escape eternal darkness and damnation. This is strong meat for My church to digest. He that hath an ear, listen to what the Spirit is saying to His church. Many are called; but few are chosen. Do you choose to be chosen? Arise, shine, for your light hath come!

My little ones, you are so very precious to Me. I know your hearts and how much you love Me and are willing to please Me. Hold fast a little longer; and My light will once again penetrate your darkness. In the beginning, was My Word; and My Word was made flesh and dwelt among you. So be it according to My Words. Isaiah 60:1-3

A song, "Oh, how He loves you and me. Oh, how He loves you and me. He sent His Son. His will be done. Oh, how He loves you. Oh, how He loves me. Oh, how He loves you and me."

Your ABBA Father.

"My Glory will shine through their faces…"

SACRIFICE
by God

"Lord? How do we sacrifice for You today, in this day? What is pleasing to You in our day?"

I have waited for you, My child, to ask this question. What is the most precious thing you have in your possession? In your case, it is time. For others, it is money. Others, material things. Others, talents (natural, not supernatural). Others, family. Did I not say, "Forsake all for Me," brothers, fathers, sisters, mothers? That means, do not put your families before Me. Love them. Sacrifice for them but for My Name's sake. I AM a jealous God.

Remember, did not Abraham offer Isaac up to Me for sacrifice?

A song, *"I surrender all. All to Jesus, I surrender. I surrender all."*

"Lord? How do we sacrifice for You today, in this day?"

MERCY
by God

Dear children, My mercy is unexplainable and indefinable because there are no words in your vocabulary to describe it.

"Please try Father."

Child, you can feel My love but not My mercy. You do not have the composite to. You are not omniscient, all-knowing, all-powerful (Trinity). I AM the potter; you are the clay. Just know that your Heavenly Father is merciful, compassionate, loving, kind-hearted, forgiving, understanding, protective, all-encompassing, long-suffering and yes, jealous of My creation. I gave you a free will to choose Me and My mercy or turn your back and live forever in depravity or corruption.

"My mercy is unexplainable..."

"...choose Me and My mercy..."

Your Merciful, Heavenly Father.

POSSESSIONS
by God

Everything I have, I have given you; so why do you still want more? Do I not clothe the lilies of the field and all of My Creation? Are they not more beautiful than words can describe? Will I not do the same for you? When I clothed you, I made you divine and put My Spirit within you - My proudest possessions. You immediately tossed it away for lesser possessions. Did I not say in My Word that I AM a most jealous God?

Give me all of your possessions; and I will give you mine. Matthew 6:33

Your Maker, your Possessor, your Father of all Mankind.

A song, *"I surrender all; I surrender all. All to Jesus I surrender. I surrender all."*

PREDESTINATION
by God

Yes, My little one, this is a big question for My church today. There is no way you can fully understand this mystery because you are not Me, Your God and Father. To Me, it is so simple; to you so complex. I knew you before your seed was implanted in your mother's womb. I knew you would choose life in Christ and have guarded you with angels before and even after your conversion. The same truth is with every soul since the beginning of time.

I AM God; and there is none other. All My Creation has and will have a chance to choose to believe My plan or not. I love each one passionately and woo each one by My Spirit. My Hand is not shortened that it cannot save and hear every cry that comes My way. My ears are always open to your cry for help.

I so desire for you to believe that your God created you and gave you a free will to choose and love Me. Please open your heart now and feel My Love. I have designed a plan that We can even be one by My Holy Spirit. He can guide you to all My Truths and has My gifts for you. You, who do not choose to believe, I knew from the beginning. Did I not say in My Word that the tares and wheat would grow together until harvest time? On your time, you too have had many opportunities to choose My plan by the way of the Cross. But you blinded Your eyes and pushed Me away many times for other gods in spite of My love. Soon your door and My door will shut; and no more grace will prevail. You will be damned forevermore.

Dear ones, We are calling to you oh, so tenderly. There is still room at the cross for you. You were not predestined for failure but made to open your hearts to your Father's calling you home. I AM your Father; and you are My prodigal son. Come home! Come home! Come home!

Many are called; but few are chosen. Do you choose to be chosen?

That, My little one, is the definition of predestination. I chose you. The question is do you choose Me? Today is the day of salvation. (Romans 9)

A song, *"There's room at the cross for you. There's room at the cross for you. There's still room for more, there's room at the cross for you."*

Jerusalem, My Namesake
by God

This land is mine. Bethlehem means the house of bread. I have My stake there. Am I not God? And there is none other.

I heal; and I kill; and I make alive. Many are called; but few are chosen. I have chosen Jerusalem and the Jewish people for My family and home forever. Do mortal men think they can destroy My inheritance without destroying Me? I AM that I AM. My Will will be done on earth as it is in Heaven. No man can say this - only Jehovah, your God.

Did I not tell you all of these things in My Word, the written Word? Heaven and earth will pass; but My Words will live on. Read Zachariah 12 and see all these things come to pass in your lifetime. Also read Revelation 21 and 22.

Our teams are winners in your game of life. Death has no victory over you, My loved ones. Your Father and My Son will come to you and guide you through into eternity. I need and want your love, praises, and blessings more now than ever before.

Your earth is disintegrating before your very eyes. What is happening all around will soon be happening in Jerusalem. She is a stumbling block for all the world because she is Mine. If the world hates her, how much more do they hate Me? Oh, My people, how they are deceived in believing the lies of Satan. With their eyes wide open, they are walking into a pit of burning flames throughout eternity. Please, My people, pray for them! Pray for their eyes to be opened before too late.

A song, *"Soon and very soon, you are going to see the Lord. Soon and very soon, you are going to see the Lord."*

Stand your ground. The battle is the Lord's. My Love is your shield and protection.

DIVINE ORDER
by God

This is the biggest mystery to mankind. No man argues this subject; because none know My exact will in these matters. Man is only finite, I AM infinite. You are not completed yet. But by My Spirit, your Father can and will show you My will and things to come. He that hath an ear can and will be in tune to My Truths. Then, blessings shall and will come forth. Yes, as you feel in your spirit and see with your eyes, things are coming forth at a fast pace.

Look up, My children, redemption is at your back door and soon will be coming through your front door. Behold! Behold! To this midnight call. Look, look around you. Can you not see the degradation coming forth, even to your doorstep now (mail), burglaries, shootings?

Now, one can truly say, "To live is for Christ and to die is gain". And as Jesus, your Savior said, "I came to minister, not to be ministered to".

Yes, I AM coming for these first.

Then all hell will break forth. More martyrs — many will give their lives for Christ.

Jews will see Me as the risen Messiah.

Back again I come with My Bride at My Side (one thousand year reign on earth). Read Revelations 21 and 22 — Holy Spirit will explain.

A song. "This is the day, this is the day that the Lord hath made, that the Lord hath made. This is the day, this is the day that the Lord hath made, that the Lord hath made. Let us rejoice and be glad in it. Let us rejoice and be glad in it. This is the day, this is the day that the Lord hath made."

THY KINGDOM COME
by God

Daughter, My Kingdom now is not of this world but soon and very soon, you will see My Kingdom break forth in all its splendor. Remember, My Son, Jesus Christ, said, "My Kingdom is not of this world," to Pontius Pilate. You, My child, too, can make this same statement for you are literally in His Kingdom now and seated in high places with Me in the supernatural Kingdom. There is a Heavenly Kingdom and an earthly kingdom. Jesus Christ will soon be in both.

Time is running out on planet Earth. The angels in Heaven and earth are excited and shouting with joy, ready to bring My Kingdom forth. There will be a great battle! But, My direction to My people is to stand! This is My battle. Watch this army (My army) come forth and fight this battle for you.

Praise! Praise! Praise Me as your other Kingdom arises from dust and ashes. As I said to King Jehoshaphat, "Stand, the battle is the Lord's". I AM also saying to My spiritual people, My Son's Body, stand and watch your Heavenly Kingdom come forth with all the splendor of eternity.

A song, *"This is the day! This is the day that the Lord hath made, that the Lord hath made. Rejoice and be glad in it, glad in it!"*

Another song, *"Hallelujah! Hallelujah! Hallelujah! Christ the Glory. Hallelujah! Amen!"*

Another song, *"The King is coming! The King is coming!"*

Another song, *"Amazing Grace, how sweet the sound!"*

The Heavens are soon to break open, My child. You will see your Savior, Jesus Christ, breaking through the clouds in all His Glory. The angels will be gathering My saints from the north, south, east, and west.

A song, "Go shout it on the mountain, that Jesus Christ is Lord. Go shout it on the mountains; go shout it on the mountains. Go shout it on the mountains that Jesus Christ is Lord."

Mother Mary
by God

I chose this young maiden to bring forth all My Glory in a human body, a baby. "Why", you ask, "Mary in particular?" Because she was or would be in sympathy with My Plan because she was humble. Remember, she said, "Let it be done according to Your Word". Also, it had been prophesied long before in Isaiah that through her blood line, this amazing event would take place. Her seed was impregnated by My Holy Spirit (that part of Me) (I AM three parts). That is why My Catholic body gives her the honor and calls her, "Mother of God."

This is not offensive to Me as some think. You see, in their minds, they are worshiping Me, not Mary. She conceived and brought forth My only begotten Son, Jesus Christ - the Anointed Savior of all mankind. I, the Father, by the Spirit, fertilized Mary's seed; and We produced an Offspring. This was a one-time event. It has never happened before and never will again.

Mary, in Heaven, is now recognized with great honor and is placed in high regard. After Us, she is given the most honor and praises and should be on earth too. Many eyes will be opened when this is finally revealed. My Son hurts and grieves constantly because of this false attitude against His mother. Think how you would feel about your mother in Heaven. My Catholic family will be blessed in Heaven and now on earth because of their devotion to Mary. She is seated in high places with Us and intercedes for all of you. Yes, there is intercession in Heaven. Can you see we are family here too? This is a Family Plan, from Adam to eternity.

I AM your Father. Mary is your Mother. And Jesus is your elder brother.

Is this too much for you to comprehend?

Selah

"I chose this young maiden to bring forth all My Glory..."

"Her seed was impregnated by My Holy Spirit...

(Jesus) Mary, My mother, also has other children (blood) in Heaven. They are My half-brothers and sisters. Joseph was My earthly father. Joseph, too, is to be remembered with high respect and honor but not on the same level as Mary. Yes, there are ranks in Heaven. Some have more authority and ranks than others.

All are in agreement; and love permeates and rules here. We are One. Duties are performed as My Holy Spirit directs. The presence of My Son, Jesus, is everywhere.

Yes, your Heavenly Father has a throne and court. Angels prevail everywhere. The act of the cross is foremost in everyone's mind; because only the Blood of Jesus opens the door to eternity (your passport). Oh, My children, your Father has a big heart and big family; and there is still room for more.

A song, *"There's still room at the cross for you. There's room at the cross for you. There's still room for more so please, open My door. There's room at the cross for you."*

"...and We produced an Offspring."

"She is seated in high places with Us and intercedes for all of you."

Janie Allen

LOVE OF GOD
by God

My Love is incomprehensible, never-ending, and has no beginning and no ending. The biggest mystery in all the universe is My unconditional Love for mankind (all). There is nothing you can do that will deny this.

Love transcends all measure. No one can explain it. It is a phenomenon. How it comes about, no one knows nor can explain. How can one fathom My love for you or yours for Me? Love is My Gift to you, believers and unbelievers of Me and My Christ. As rain comes down to shower the earth, so My Love falls to melt your hearts. One cannot see it, smell it, or taste it, for it is like a consuming fire and will melt your heart. You have a choice to turn it off or let it consume you. My Love can melt cold, cold hearts as nothing else. Amazingly, it can also be passed on or become stagnant in you. Some are willing to let Me love them more than others and choose to share My Love and tell others about Me.

As you imagine, there are dimensions and types of My Love for you and you for each other. Your words are romantic and passionate for courtship love. Yes, this is of Me for procreation. It has rules and regulations and is a beautiful love if done by My guidelines.

Another kind of love is compassionate, caring, full of empathy and sympathy, enduring, and expressed with gratitude. These attributes are Mine to share with My Creation. (I Corinthians 13)

A song, *"Love makes the world go round; love makes the world go round. God sent His Son. His Will be done. Love makes the world go round."*

Love is long-suffering, enduring, patient, gentle, and serving. There is a mystery ingredient; but you do not have a word for it. There is not a word in your language for it. This, My child, is a mystery of creation.

Your Agape Father.

"My Love is incomprehensible, never-ending, and has no beginning and no ending."

DIVINE CONCEPTION
by God

My Ways are not your ways; and yours are not always mine. This concept is hard to understand as are many of My Ways. My Utmost Plan is for Us to be One in mind, body, and spirit. When this comes about and does take place, there is new birth born of the Spirit, born from above, born of the Spirit, out of My love. Also, another concept emerges. This is when My Creation (man and woman) become one. Human birth can come forth. Can you see that parallel?

All life comes from a seed. The Spiritual is the seed of My Word. I AM the Living Word. The Natural seed is the love between man and woman. Eros love brings forth the human seed between them. This is the concept of reproduction. Natural seed produces unregenerate man (natural man). Spiritual seed produces Christians (spiritual or supernatural man). When a Christian is impregnated with My Seed or when a man or woman is impregnated with My Seed, a new Birth occurs. A Divine Nature can produce another Divine race. This, My Child, is a Divine Concept.

When we are one, more sons come forth. When the human race becomes one - more children. Christians begat Christians (people).

When My Son was conceived, Mary became One with My Spirit. The hypostatic union came forth. His Name was Jesus Christ, Son of Man and Son of God, Emmanuel. That was Divine Conception.

A song, *"Love makes the world go 'round. Love makes the world go 'round. He sent His Son; the world He won. Love makes the world go 'round."*

Another song, *"This is your story; this is your song - loving your Savior, all the day long."*

Christmas is Our Love Story, yours and Mine.

THE JEW
by God

I have engraved them on the palm of My Hand. From Abraham to today, My Hand has been on My people - the Jewish nation. I birthed them, then rescued them, and through much difficulty they advanced to Jerusalem. My Name and My Stamp is on them and on My land. I have My stake there. And my, what a battle to keep it there.

My little ones, I love all My Creation. I want them to know Me and My way to Me through the cross, the Blood sacrifice of My Son the Messiah.

These, My people, are the ones I chose to illustrate this. That is the reason for all their attacks by Satan. He is their enemy from the beginning. To destroy them is his intention. He uses mankind to do this. When they turn to Me and seek My Face, I always come to their rescue individually and corporately.

They are a stubborn people and try all measures before seeking Me. Oh, how I love them with a father's heart; and you must too. I know who will and who will not repent. This breaks My Heart. I also know the end from the beginning. All Israel will be saved when I create in them a new heart and a broken spirit when they turn toward Me. I will push their enemy aside with one sweep of My Hand and breathe on them with My Spirit. Then I will be their God; and they will be My People. They will recognize My Son, their anointed Messiah, the King of Kings and Lord of Lords. (Ezekiel 34 - 37 and Jeremiah 27-31)

"I want them to know Me and My way to Me through the cross..."

Peace
by God

My Child! My Peace I give unto you, not as the world giveth unto you. Let not your heart be troubled, neither let it be afraid. In the world you will have tribulation. In Me only, will you have Peace.

Let not your heart be troubled; neither let it be afraid. I in you, you in Me, and we are in our Father, God Almighty. Remember, when I walked the earth I spoke Peace to all I contacted. Confusion, troubles, and misunderstandings all melt away when I impart My Peace on you. Now I AM telling all of you to receive My Peace. Peace is from within, not without. Even when and if your whole world blows up, you can still feel and have My Peace. My Peace I leave with you, not as the world gives you.

Let not your heart be troubled, nor be afraid. Stand and watch your salvation burst forth right before your very eyes. Not thousands, but millions are being saved all around your world. You are My voice. Let no one you know or that I bring into your presence be left without your prayers. These happenings are not by chance. Only by the fruits of My Spirit will this generation hear My Voice and be saved.

Love, Joy, Peace, Long Suffering, Gentleness, Goodness, Kindness.

The world wants this, not religion. Russia is still open. China is open to Me now. As My Christmas season approaches let love, joy, and peace prevail. Your world is crying for peace; but only in hearts can peace prevail. Open your hearts; and let Me give you My Peace. Peace = Eternal Stability and Security. (John 14, 16, and Romans 8)

"...the Church (My Church) is hurting."

THE HURTING CHURCH
by God

My child (and that you are), when your heart is broken, Mine is too. Yes My child, the Church (My Church) is hurting. Not because of you, but because they have not obeyed My Spiritual Laws.

'Do ye one to another as you would have them do unto you.'

This Law of Mine is being ignored in My Body. Also, the Head of My Church is Jesus Christ, not the leading minister of any denominational church. Much distress has come forth because of this principle. I work through man; but man must stay under Divine Order.

Christ is the Head. Man is always just mere man without the leading of the Holy Spirit. I AM setting this Divine Order back in order (the Kingdom of God with My King on the Throne).

When My pastors humble themselves and seek My Face, I will put the Church back in its place. Until then, My sheep will be scattered and wandering from place to place seeking a home but finding none. Hold on a little while; and this situation will change suddenly. Grace will find its place in My Kingdom.

You, My children, are My daughters and sons of Grace, born of the Spirit of Grace. When My shepherds want to be one with My family of Grace, much healing will take place.

At this time, the Church is going through much persecution. Unity is coming forth. Forgiveness is required. And Love is shed abroad for each and all by My Holy Spirit. I command you that you love one another as I have loved you, that all will know that Christ is My Son.

Just ask, and I will give you the Love.

Your Loving Father.

"...the Church is going through much persecution."

Man

by God

Man is the object of My Affection. What is man that I AM mindful of him? Am I not a loving God? Did I not need a love object? So I made one out of My earth and called Him Adam (Adam equals clay or earth).

I AM is the Creator of Heaven and Earth. I AM is the origin of man. You did not evolve. You did not just appear from nowhere. You were created by a Divine Hand. God breathed in a special way and Life began. Then appeared man.

My man then was perfect, no defects. Now there are defects in man, all because of your free will. My children, I had to do this. This is the most important Gift (free will) I have ever given you. Until the End, it shall remain.

It is given at your birth along with your genes. Just notice it in a newborn baby. He can choose to cry or not to cry. This one Gift of your Father is what makes the Kingdom of God a loving Family.

First, you choose Me through My Son by way of the cross. Then I command you to love one another as I have loved you. This, My child, is your strongest commandment. You do not have too much of a choice here; for if you choose not to, you wither and die on the vine. Yes, you are still in My Family of God; but your light does not shine. Oh, how I wish My Family could digest this one morsel. Only one word in your language keeps this Love from coming forth (unforgiveness).

Remember, My children, all you have to do is ask Me; and I will forgive you. Judas, the Lord Jesus' disciple, never asked.

1 John 1:9 "If we confess our sins, He is faithful and just to forgive us our sins, and to cleanse us from all unrighteousness."

A song, *"Trust and obey, for there's no other way to be happy in Jesus, but to trust and obey."*

Another song, *"What a friend we have in Jesus. What a friend we have in Jesus. Take it to the Lord in prayer."*

You were made in My Image (the Image of God- body, soul, spirit). Look at Jesus. He is My Image (Icon) = picture of Me. That's why we feel familiar with each other. That's why we can homogenize so well. Just like milk — the cream is the Holy Spirit.

You have your Father's make up (eyes, nose, mouth, hands, two legs, fingers). You are wonderfully and fearfully made. (Psalms 139)

Truly a miracle composite, even if I do say so Myself. You are My Masterpiece! (Psalm 8)

Soul Sleep
by God

My child, have you ever even thought along these lines?

You know you are a composite (body, soul, and spirit). Also, you know your soul = your mind = your emotions and your will. When one is absent from the body and present with the Lord, it is referred to as soul sleep. This is what takes place in your dream life, somewhat. You do not have a body; but you are still functioning.

"This is very deep for me, Lord, to grasp."

I know, My sweet little one, but I can give you celestial thoughts and pictures for you to understand. Part of your mind never sleeps. This is your dream world. Your body is immobile at this time (semi-paralyzed).

As I have said before, Man is wonderfully and fearfully made (Psalms 8 and 139). You are My masterpiece. I could and can control you, but not even in your sleep do I try. The Holy Spirit is your control; and He is fed by you (Selah). When your body and mind separate from your spirit; this equals soul sleep (death). Your spirit never sleeps or dies. Your body can appear and disappear "whenever", like Jesus' did when He was resurrected. Now this takes place for you in Heaven, but not on earth unless I desire for this to happen. Remember Moses and Elijah on the mountain with Peter, James, and John. The disciples recognized Moses and Elijah and even talked to them. Your Father God has no limitations. Only man has limitations.

Remember Paul struggled to get out of his body. He realized his body had limitations. My dear child, your body holds you back. It is only your tent and is destructible. Your mind and spirit are much more important. Feed your mind on Me; and My Words and your spirit will do the rest.

"The Spirit itself beareth witness with our spirit, that we are children of God: And if children, then heirs; heirs of God, and joint-heirs with Christ; if so be that we suffer with Him, that we may be also glorified together." (Romans 8:16)

When you come to Me, the Spirit has control of your mind. That is soul sleep.

P.S. Have I not said that if you want information, just ask Me?

PROVISIONS
by God

Ephesians 6, Proverbs 3

My child, I know you think these are unusual headlines; but these are unusual days for My Divine ones - those born of My Spirit, born from above, born of the Spirit, out of My Love. Clouds are forming in every direction. Storms, earthquakes, and hurricanes are reported in all the earth. But your Father God told you about all of this many eons ago in the Word of God.

Yes, you are in the very end.

That is why you need Me and My provisions. I knew all of this from the beginning and have provided provisions for you in this age. Fear is your worst enemy. Did not My Son, Jesus Christ, say "Fear Not" to all He talked to? "Fear Not" is what He is still saying today.

If We made you from the beginning, We can surely provide for you until you are in Our Bosoms (literally). Now you have the blood of Christ and the Holy Spirit of the Trinity to give you foreknowledge, discernment, and many other gifts to warn you and protect and heal you. Don't forget to always call on My angels who are ever ready to minister (flashlight).

Proverbs 3:5-6, "Trust in the Lord with all thine heart; and lean not unto thine own understanding. In all thy ways acknowledge Him, and He shall direct thy paths."

Can you see you can be wound up in My cocoon in time of trouble?

Signed, El SHADDAI.

GUILT
by God

1Cor. 10:13 "There hath no temptation taken you but such as is common to man: but God is faithful, who will not suffer you to be tempted above that ye are able; but will with the temptation also make a way to escape, that ye may be able to bear it."

My child, temptations are always coming to My beloved Saints. Remember they came to Me daily. I was flesh and blood, too. I had the Holy Spirit too, just as you do.

In My Word, it is revealed that satan will leave for a season.

Children, you will not always pass your temptations because you are not Me. This is where guilt enters. Remember Adam and Eve? They too, experienced guilt. This is not all bad, but you must turn to Me and be released from it. (1 John 1:9) I love you with a father's love and always will forgive you if your heart is right. You have to ask Me first and confess your failings. We knew you from the beginning. My Son will always set you free of that old spirit of guilt. Guilt is paralyzing and a menace to your very soul. You are bound and tied up until the Son sets you free.

"If the Son therefore shall make you free, ye shall be free indeed." John 8:36

Guilt is your enemy; and freedom is your friend.

Beloved, you are Mine. I bought you with a price. Now you will and can be My Prize to all mankind. Can't you see what a special gift you are to Me and to others when you are released from that old dragon of guilt?

From the One who loves you the most,

Your Daddy, Agape.

"I will always forgive you."

Song

by God

A song, *"In my heart there rings a melody, of heaven's harmony, rings a melody of heaven's harmony today."*

Yes, My little ones, I have put melodies in all of you in the form of poetry and music (writers, composers). Even My other creations sing to Me - the birds, the porpoises, the whales, and many others (even monkeys). I have made My creation to worship Me in many ways; but Song is the highest of praise to your Father God.

Also, it quickens you as well as Me. Your body is refreshed as well as Mine. Depression is lifted; frowns turn into smiles. You are happy as well as am I. Please never let your enemy take and pluck the spirit of Song and singing from your heart. Your Father put it there at your birth and desires for it to stay until you meet Me face to face. Then I will put a new song in your heart. I even said in My Word, I will give you a new song (Revelation).

Also, one last reminder, satan leaves when you are singing love songs and praise and worship to Me.

"Father, did Jesus sing?"

Yes, daughter, all the time and still sings even through eternity.

"Father, do You sing?"

I AM is the Creator and author of songs. So what do you think?

A song, *"Oh, how I love Jesus. Oh, how I love Jesus. Oh, how I love Jesus, because He first loved me."*

Even the flowers and trees like My Music.

Another song, *"I love to tell the story of Jesus and His Love. The old, old story of Jesus and His Love."* (Zephaniah 3: 17)

DEATH
by God

I Cor. 15:55 Hebrews 2

"O DEATH WHERE IS THY STING? O GRAVE WHERE IS THY VICTORY?"

The sting of sin is death. The victory of the grave is life in the Vine. Yes, for you who know Me as your Father (Daddy, Abba) God (through the provisions of My Son and His Blood) death has no sting. This passing can be oh so sweet if you choose it this way and oh so miserable if you let Jesus pass you by. Jesus is your Vine; and you are His Branches - so abide in Him through My Word, communion, meditation, thought, and through memory.

"O taste and see that the Lord is good..." (Psalm 34:8)

I AM never away from you at any time, here or there, awake or asleep. Remember, your Father created you and can surely provide for you even through the death process. Oh child, please come to Me. Lean on Me; and let Me be your burden bearer. You are so fragile; but I AM so strong.

A song, *"Jesus loves me, this I know; for the Bible tells me so. Little ones to Him belong. We are weak; but He is strong.*

Now you are asking Me, "What about those left behind?" Can I not hold their hand in their time of distress? Can I not be their Father, too? Can I not provide for them in every way?

I AM still their Father. Did I not send My Holy Spirit to them to keep them in all their ways?

A song, *"Only believe. Only believe. All things are possible when you believe."*

"The Spirit itself beareth witness with our spirit, that we are children of God: And if children, then heirs; heirs of God, and joint-heirs with Christ; if so be that we suffer with Him, that we may be also glorified together." (Romans 8:16-17)

Please, My child, hold on to the lifeline, your Vine; for you are My overcomers. I love you oh so tenderly. Didn't I pluck My Heart out so you could have all of Me forever? Your Divine Father to His Divine Children.

PRECIOUS METALS
by God

A song, "Only believe. Only believe. All things are possible, only believe."

My people, My loved ones, I AM showering My people with not only showers of blessings but showers of gold and silver and many other precious metals. Begin to look for them wherever My Glory falls. Yes! Dance and worship will bring My Glory down.

Haven't I said in My Word that all that I have is yours if all that you have is mine (body, soul, and Spirit, all your possessions, but mainly your will). Can you say, My child, "I am willing to do your will, Father"? My will is for you to love your God with all your heart, mind, and soul and love your neighbor as thyself. All other laws will fall in place. (Jesus is teaching on the beatitudes.) This should be your attitude.

As you want to give showers of blessings to your children, so do I. As you desire for them to be prosperous, so do I. As you leave your precious metal (gold and silver) for their inheritance and even part with them beforehand, so do I. Yes! I AM showering My precious metals here with you there before you depart and come hither. This is only a preview of what your total inheritance will be. It's impossible for you to fathom the love of your Heavenly Father. Selah

A song, *"Oh, how I love Jesus. Oh, how I love Jesus. Oh, how I love Jesus; because He first loved me."*

REPRIEVE AND REPENTANCE
by God

"Lord, are you holding back your judgments right now in the world? Are you holding back the end of the end times that we all thought that we were in?"

Yes, My true and faithful one, I have put your world on hold for a temporary time. You have been given a reprieve for repentance. I have heard your cries and have seen your tears and felt your heart beat over your trials and tribulations and have changed the course of direction for a short period of time (yours, not mine).

I'm not on your time clock. USA and Israel have been given a reprieve; because I have heard your prayers and theirs. My heart and your Father's heart have been warmed and touched when He hears and sees His family on their knees. Oh, the love we have for you. If you could only know and feel and then repent. You say, "Repent from what?"

I AM "says" - "from your lackadaisical attitude of Me and My Family here, My Son, the Messiah and all others."

Do you ever think of what is next? It is all in My Word. Repent from not reading My Word. Do you realize it is alive and anointed, more so than your daily newspaper or your U.S. News & World Report? Yes. Read those. But read Me first. When you finish with the Bible, My daily news, you are in a positive direction. With others, like the newspaper, you are left hanging.

Oh, how I want you to know Me and love Me intimately. You are My Divine ones; born from the Spirit, born from above, born from the Spirit, out of My Love.

YOUR ABBA FATHER, YOUR DADDY.

A song, *"Oh, how I love Jesus. Oh, how I love Jesus. Oh, how I love Jesus; because He first loved me."*

Another song, *"Oh, how He loves you and me. Oh, how He loves you and me. He sent His Son; His will be done. Oh, how He loves you! Oh, how He loves me. Oh, how He loves you and me."*

Look Up (Redemption)
by God

A song, *"Coming again. Coming again. It may be evening, it may be night; but Jesus is coming again."*

Another song, *"Jesus may come in the morning. Jesus may come at noon. Jesus may come in the evening; so keep your heart in tune."*

Yes, My Church (Iglesia where it means "called out one"), look up. Your redemption draweth nigh. Why do all of you continue to look downward? My Reign now is in the Heavenly Realm. The Kingdom of God is neither meat nor drink but love, joy, and peace in the Holy Spirit.

A song, *"This is your story; this is your song- praising your Savior all the day long."*

Another song, *"In my heart, there rings a melody, rings a melody of Heaven's harmony. In my heart there rings a melody, rings a melody to stay."*

Keep singing, My children, for then your Spirit and mine too, are lifted and lightened. If you only knew what singing does to your whole body. My songs and music are uplifting. Satan's are demonic and downgrading (depressing). Many souls are lost because of his music.

Yes little ones, you redeemed ones, your redemption is just around one more corner. Hold fast to your lifeline, Jesus Christ and My Holy Spirit. These two can bring you through to My splendor and magnitude of eternal divinity, seated in heavenly places with Me (Us) throughout eternity.

Please hold on for dear life. We will never leave you.

YOUR AGAPE FATHER.

A song, *"Holy! Holy! Holy! Lord God Almighty."*

Janie Allen

THE CRUCIFIXION
by God

"From the Cross to the Crown"

My Bride, always at My side, I want to tell you the truth about Me and your journey from the cross to the grave to the crown. You are Mine. Oh, how precious you are to Me, My sweetheart. Your smell is perfume to My soul. Your tender heart is like an arrow piercing mine and dividing it for all of you. Your smile in My direction is like a thousand sunrises. Your love is as brilliant as a thousand sunsets. Your prayers, I keep in My bosom constantly. Your songs keep My feet in perfect harmony. Your dance inspires My every longing for our day of celebration, our wedding day - a day of rejoicing, singing, praising, dancing, and fulfilling our Oneship. You in Me and I in you, abiding with Our Father and Our Sweet, Sweet Holy Spirit.

This is your final destination from the cross to the crown (yours and Mine). Our Easter story. Yours and Mine.

A song, *"This is the day, this is the day that the Lord hath made, that the Lord hath made. I will rejoice. I will rejoice and be glad in it and be glad in it."*

Another song, *"Oh, what a beautiful morning. Oh, what a beautiful day. Everything is going my way."*

Your King to His Queen With Divine Love, Jesus.

A song (Near to the Heart of God by Cleveland McAfee),

> *"There is a place of quiet rest, near to the heart of God, a place where sin cannot molest, near to the heart of God. O Jesus, blessed Redeemer, sent from the heart of God. Hold us who wait before thee, near to the heart of God. There is a place of comfort sweet, near*

to the heart of God; a place where we and our Savior meet, near to the heart of God. O Jesus, blessed Redeemer, sent from the heart of God. Hold us who wait before thee, near to the heart of God. There is a place of full release, near to the heart of God; a place where all is joy and peace, near to the heart of God."

Attitude Equals the Beatitude
by God

Yes, My dear little one, your attitude is your life pattern. If anyone desires to know My attitude, just look up the Sermon on the Mount. You call them the Beatitudes. I call them your attitudes, yours and Mine. Yes, these are so very hard to digest. In the past, most of My children have just skipped over them saying, "Oh me, these are not for me. No way could I fulfill them."

But now I want you to take a second look at Matthew 5 and 6.

Yes, My church (My called out ones), these are written for you (My own) today. Yes, you can fulfill these attitudes; because I have provided you with My Holy Spirit. He is your Enabler to do so. Activate Him. All you need to do so, is desire and want to do My Will. Will to do My "will", and He will do it for you. Just act it out; and watch Him perform in every case.

You say, "Oh my! Are you sure, Father?"

I say, try Me and My ways and see. I will give you My wisdom, My understanding, My love, My strength, My Power (all of the seven-fold ministries of My Holy Spirit) to fulfill your life in the vine. Jesus Christ is your pattern. As mortals say, "You are a chip off the same (old) block."

My dear ones, My own, I have faith in you. All I desire is your will. Will you release your will and be free to take up Mine? This attitude is your priority.

Resurrection Day
by God

A song, *"Oh, what a beautiful morning! Oh, what a beautiful day! Everything is going my way."*

Another song, *"This is the day, this is the day that the Lord has made, that the Lord has made."*

A song, *"He lives! He lives! He lives within my heart. I know He lives. I know because He lives within my heart."*

Another song, *"Up from the grave He arose, like a mighty warrior He arose. He arose! He arose!"*

A song, *"There is a river that comes from deep within. There is a river that cleanses us from all sin."*

Another song, *"My heart cries for you; my heart died for you. Please come back to Me."*

My called out ones, you are My passion. Can you believe this? I AM passionately in love with all of you to the extent that I gave My heart, My blood, the cross at Calvary to replace it with your love for Me, your passion for Me. My Bride, tell Me how much you love and cherish Me today.

A song, *"My heart cries for you. My heart dies for you. Just to hear your voice is oh so tender to My ears."*

Remember I AM man, too. I have feelings; I have wants. I can still cry, laugh, feel pain, and leap for joy. I want to walk with you, talk with you, and tell you, you are My own. So please come to My Garden alone.

A song, *"My Heart dies for you; My heart cries for you."*

Read Song of Solomon. You are My Bride. Always, I desire you by My side.

A song, *"Soon and very soon you are going to see your Lord. Soon and very soon, you are going to see your Lord."*

Are you as excited as I am? Don't let the world put you into their spin. Don't let the world swallow you up with grit from within. Don't be so earthly minded that you can't see and taste and smell Heaven. Heaven is at your door. You have My permission to open and come in.

Revelation 3. Behold, I stand at your door. Knock and it shall be opened to you; seek and you shall find. Your resurrection day, yours and Mine — this is the day our Father has made, yours and Mine.

A song, *"Oh, how He loves you and me. He sent His Son, His will be done. Oh, how He loves you, oh how He loves me."*

Come see, come see! The tomb is empty.

Knowing God
by God

Yes, My daughter, knowing Me is loving Me. Remember when I said in My Word (Bible), "They never knew Me."

This passage is always confusing to My children. You say, "How can they use My name and do My work and not know Me?"

And I say, "It is possible."

"Tell me Lord."

Seeking My face and My presence is to know Me. Remember St. Paul said, "Lord, I want to know you and the power of Your Resurrection and the fellowship of Your suffering, even into the conformity of Your death." Paul truly knew Me. Remember, he also said, "For to me to live is Christ, and to die is gain." My children, St. Paul knew Me and knows Me.

Children, there are degrees in knowing Me. My little ones know Me because they have fewer hindrances. Religion is a force that hinders many of My people. Oh so many other things creep in to replace Me. Remember My commandments. You shall have no other gods; and you shall love the Lord your God with all your heart, mind, and soul and your neighbor as yourself. This is all I have required of My Saints in the past; but now I tell you, you are to seek My face. Look at Me, towards Me. Feel My Presence. Desire My intervention in your daily walk. Walk with Me. Talk to Me. Listen to My directions.

"O taste and see that the Lord is good..." (Psalm 34)

A song, *"I come to the Garden alone while the dew is still on the roses."*

Minister to My Son. Praise His Holy Name! Tell Him how much you love Him for giving His Blood to bring you into My Presence.

Oh, My children, these are unusual days and times you are confronting. Unless you know Me and My Presence, you will not make it. Your enemy stalks about as a roaring lion. But My Holy Spirit is omniscient, all-powerful, all-knowing, and everywhere. My angels are on call and are guarding My knowing ones. Do you want to know Me or don't you? This is My question.

A song, *"Lord, I want to know you; look upon your face. Lord, I want to know you, to feel Your Grace."*

Another song, *"Thank you, Lord, for saving my soul. Thank you, Lord, for making me whole."*

"Desire My intervention in your daily walk."

Marriage: Human and Divine
by God

Marriage, My little one, is of your Father God. The pattern is from My Family here in Heaven. You remember that Moses got the pattern for the tabernacle from the One here in heaven. So I'm giving you the pattern for marriage.

There is an earthly marriage and a heavenly marriage. I AM getting a Bride through My Holy Spirit. I, Your Heavenly Father, wifed Israel and brought forth My son, Jesus, by the Holy Spirit through Mary. And now, the Holy Spirit is also bringing forth His Bride. I have never left or betrayed My wife, Israel. She departed from Me. But soon and very soon, she will return and will run with open arms to My only Divine Son, her brother and King.

It is an old saying, but true. "She is the apple of My Eye." Oh, how I love her and am wooing and calling her back to Me. Yes, I will show her Jesus; and how she will mourn and cry and weep because of her wrongdoing. Yes, I have forgiven her; but she has not forgiven Me. She is still too proud and self-sufficient. She wants My Love but doesn't want to repent. And yet, soon and very soon, she is going to see her Lord.

A song, *"Soon and very soon, she is going to see her Lord. Soon and very soon, she is going to see her Lord."*

Now, My little one, about human marriage - I made man and then woman from man and performed the first marriage. The Bible begins and ends with My two marriages. It begins with human and ends with Divine. Human marriage brings forth and populates My Kingdom for Me (the Kingdom of God). As birth pains bring forth human births, so do spiritual birth pains bring forth divine births. (Isaiah 62 and Isaiah 66). Labor is required for both. Nurturing is required for both. Children are children in the heavenly Kingdom and also in the earthly Kingdom. Love is also in both (unconditional). Without it, neither Kingdom would survive.

Satan has make a mock of earthly marriage - marred it, torn it asunder, almost destroyed it completely. But in

My Word, I say, "At the end of time they will still be given away in marriage." Satan will not and cannot win. He is a defeated foe and knows it.

My Bride loves Me now; and I know it. My Father knows it too, and is waiting for her to dress herself in her fine linen pure white robe and run to Me with all heart, body, and soul. Oh, how beautiful she is making herself just to please Me. Oh, how sweet her perfume is! Oh, how beautiful her eyes are - wide open and staring in My direction. Oh, how long have I waited for this moment to love and caress her and tell her she is all Mine to have and behold forever. Oh, what a wonderful day it will be for you and Me.

My Hand is on you, My Bride, to bring you to My side where you will reside through all eternity. As Adam is not complete without his bride, Eve, I AM not complete without Mine. This, My little one, is the complete picture of marriage, the human and Divine. You have been in training for reigning. You are My Queen; and I AM your King. Heaven and earth will emerge and become One. Marriage equals Oneness. We are One; and you will be One in Us - your Trinity.

A song, *"Oh, how tenderly He is calling, calling for you and for me. Oh, so tenderly He is calling, calling for you and for me."*

Another song, *"Come home, come home! Jesus is calling us home!"*

Another song, *"Love makes the world go round. Love makes the world go round. He sent His Son; His Will be done. Love makes the world go round."*

MIDNIGHT CALL
by God

My child! My child! If you only knew what is to take place in 2002. But this is not for you to know. Because then your trust and faith would not be needed. Yes, indeed, this is what I AM requiring of you at this moment.

A song, *"Trust and obey. For there's no other way to be happy in Jesus, but to trust and obey."*

As you are hearing the distant noise of firecrackers popping to celebrate twelve o'clock midnight on planet earth, I AM getting ready for My twelve o'clock midnight call for all to repent and cry out to Me from here to there to eternity. My child, so soon and very soon, you're going to see your Lord. Are you dressed properly in your robe of righteousness? Is your cup running over? Do you have on your white linen robe? Is My white stone on your finger? Have you shod your feet with the gospel of Peace or are you, like Cinderella, losing your shoe? Are your eyes like dove eyes, only for Me? Do you have on your breastplate of righteousness? Are you ready to fight with My Sword of the Holy Spirit? Please don't forget your helmet of salvation. To put it bluntly My little one, just try Me on for size. I can fit into everyone who asks. For I AM your everything. I AM your all. I AM your everything, both great and small.

A song, *"I am your everything, I am your all. I am your everything, both great and small."* I love you, one and all.

Another song, *"This is my story; this is my song. Loving My children all the day long."*

All I have is yours. For you are all I have that is of importance to Me. My creation is the utmost on My Mind at this time.

Souls have to be snatched out of the fire in 2002. There is so much work for all of you to do. I have given you the keys to My Kingdom and your password is Jesus. These keys will open all doors to eternity, love, joy, peace, long suffering, goodness, faith, and My gifts too. All are yours. Just ask and see. Your Bridegroom (Jesus

Christ) has stepped out of His Doors and is coming forth quickly. Keep your lamps burning brightly to light His path for His soon return. Your birth pains will deliver souls for My Glory.

A song, *"Soon and very soon, you're going to see your Lord and King."*

He sends His love and kisses. Your Loving God!

The Brain
by God

Our brain is unexplainable. No man can conceive the mechanism of this so-called unit, the brain. Words, My child, are not in your vocabulary or anyone else's, but I will try. (I received a vision of a watch in my mind.) Yes, My child, there is a comparison. It has a life span. It runs for a while and then stops, just like mankind. When it stops, it needs to be repaired, just like mankind. It has many parts, just like your brain. Each one is designed for a specific purpose. When one is amiss or over-wound, it is taken to the watch maker (Me), for I AM your brain maker. Your brain is somewhat similar to mine, but not altogether. Your brain stores many memories, some good and some bad. I AM God (Almighty), omnipotent, omniscient, and all powerful. You are not. Your brain is controlled by three elements: your will, My will, or satan's will. You have a choice. When you choose My way or will (Biblical truths); that is when our brains are somewhat similar.

The soulish brain is a rebellious brain or mind. Humanist ways (I) are on your mind (brain). I want. I will. I can. But I say, "Let this mind be in you, the mind (brain) of Christ." My little one, this is our secret, yours and mine. My people can lock into this divine mind of the Godhead - Father, Son, and Holy Spirit. Not at all times, but most of you know My mind pretty well. The Holy Word (Bible) is My brain written out in words that can be understood by My counterpart (Holy Spirit). When My Son, your Savior, is asked to come and live in your heart (body), you have a ticking bomb inside of you (like a watch). My power in you is explosive. Just like a watch, you can turn it off (take it off) or turn it on. Would you My children like to wear My watch all the time? Your Father Time, Jehovah Your God.

A song, "I am your everything. I am your all."

Ps: Love is healing to any brain.

"My Glory is My Presence."

GLORY

by God

My Glory is My Presence. Where I AM; there is My Glory. You, My child, can feel My glory even now because you have been in the presence of the Godhead. To the human mind, it is unexplainable. To the Divine Mind, it is glorious. You can see, taste, and feel My Glory. You see it on someone else. You taste it in your taste buds. You feel it in your body, soul, and spirit.

A song, *"It's raining again in the Kingdom of God; it's raining on His Children."*

Another song, *"See My Glory! See My Glory! See My Glory come down."*

Yes, it does come down. I AM in control of My Glory. It is Mine to share and behold. As you know, My little one, My Presence is glorious!

Soon and sooner than your mind can grasp, My Glory will come and remain on planet earth for all to come under this canopy of My Love and Glory.

A song, *"It's beginning to snow and rain, rain in the Kingdom once again."*

Oh My Children, please close your umbrella. Let it fall on your faces and warm your hearts and quicken your steps. Now is the time for this generation to fall upon your face and seek repentance, to make ready for all I have spoken to you about. (Repentance and then, Glory.) Your Forgiving Father, to all — Each and Everyone, Love and Kisses.

BAPTISMS
by God

My little one, in your vocabulary, there are many kinds of baptisms. In My vocabulary, there are only three. St. John baptized Jesus in the River Jordan for readiness to send Him into ministry. In essence it is a symbol of death, burial, and resurrection. Also, this is to show you the way of My Pattern of a new beginning for your life. The Spirit enters to give you more power against your enemies - satan and all his cohorts. There is a world of power in the name of Jesus. Yes!

Some souls are saved without this type of baptism.

Remember, I AM God and with Me all things are possible. I love all My Creations; and I want them to have eternal life with Me. Also, I can look into hearts; and you cannot. You are finite and can only see their fruit. Remember the two criminals on the cross with Jesus? One did; and one did not. Jesus saw their hearts and said to one, "This day you will be with me in Paradise." No time for earthly baptism.

Also, another kind of baptism I would like you to write about is a baptism with fire (the fire of My Love for you and all mankind). This kind of baptism is only for the believers to enable them to live a life on earth somewhat similar to the pattern Jesus left for them - to have the boldness of Peter, divine love like St. John's, a willingness to die for the cause like St. James, and an ability to know My Heart as St. Paul. Remember how he was as Saul of Tarsus. Oh, children, there is so very much I could say about this baptism of fire (Pentecost baptism) as on the day of Pentecost. Some evidence of this kind of baptism has been around all through the church age and is described in modern history books. Even in Columbus' day, many Catholic nuns received My Baptism of Fire and Love. Satan has fought tooth and nail to blind My people from the Power and Love of this second blessing just as he has blinded My Family (Jews) from all of Me - the Father, the Son, and the Holy Spirit. Since 1900, this has changed; and My Son is now on the road of return. I AM giving My Glory and My Anointing to My precious overcomers and prayer warriors to harvest the crops and bring in the foals.

It is raining down manna in the Kingdom of God to do this.

A song, *"There is a Balm in Gilead to heal the sin sick souls. There is a Balm in Gilead to make the wounded whole."*

PS. Look up! Your redemption is drawing nigh.

From All of Us: The Father, The Son, The Holy Spirit.

SALVATION
by God

"Salvation is of the Lord," sayeth the Lord.

My sheep hear My Voice; and I know them. Another, they will not follow. There is no other way into the fold or door but by Me; for I AM your Way, Truth, and Life Eternal. I come to you that you will have life and have it more abundantly.

There is another way that seems right unto man; but it is not. For without Me in your plan, it is fraudulent or dead. I alone can give you eternal life. You are My Creation. I give you a free will - a free choice to hear My Voice (your Father's) or turn a deaf ear to My call, a free will to love Me or push Me aside. I gave you My Holy Word (your recipe - your Bible written by My Holy Spirit, inspired by Holy men of old) to believe or disbelieve.

For you who want Me as Father and My Son as your Savior through the cross, you are My Inheritance. All I have is yours. Just ask and see. I give you Eternal life, here and now and later too. Oh, how I want to pour out My love on you now. Why wait until later? All I ask of you is for you to believe that I sent Jesus to die in your place for fallen mankind. My Holy Spirit can show and explain My Plan in full detail. My Son's Blood is your covering from sins past and future. Apply it on your heart and even your doorposts as the Israelites did in the olden days. When the other spiritual world sees the sign of the cross, all evil will depart your house (literally and spiritually). Also, I will give you Divine angelic protection for you and your loved ones.

Just ask Me.

I have many gifts awaiting My inheritance. Just ask. Ask for more, My Children. Your Father is so full of love for you at this time on your time clock that He wants to load you with ammunition and fortification for all soon coming events on His time clock. His banner over you is love, love, love!

Please ask for more of My Holy Spirit to show you the way of Salvation. My Son, Jesus, is your precious Gift of My Love for you, Janie, and all mankind in this world and the next. He is with you even now to hold and lead you through this midnight hour of darkness into eternal brightness where there exists no sorrow or pain. Please give Him room in your heart to lead the way into life (eternal).

A song, *"Jesus, You're the sweetest name I know. You're just the same as Your lovely name."*

Then I said, "I love You because You first loved Me. You paid my redemption at Calvary."

Another song *"At the cross, at the cross, where I first saw the light."*

A song, *"There is no secret what God can do. What He's done for others, He'll do for you. With hearts wide open, He'll pardon you. What He's done for others, He'll do for you."*

"I love all of you passionately."

War Cry ("War" then "Peace") Part One
by God

A song, *"Thine eyes have seen the Glory of the Coming of the Lord."*

These two words (War, Peace) are the focus of all mankind in your time clock. Planet Earth is compared to a time bomb; and time is ticking out. Open your eyes and ears and listen to its ticking. The cry of war is heard in all directions - physical equals spiritual - good versus evil. Demons have been released from the pit of hell and are running to and fro to capture all, if possible. But My Holy Spirit is still available. When My people cry out (War Cry) to Me, their Maker and God, I hear and intervene in their behalf. My timing is inevitable. The climax is upon you, one and all.

They cry out, "Peace! Peace!". And no one has peace. My Peace is within. Did I not say, in the world you would have tribulation? In Me only, is true Peace. I love all of you passionately.

Did I not say I would be with you until the end? Have I not been with you since your beginning; and I will never, never leave you? Fear not, little flock, the ending is near. That is when new life really begins. My Peace I give unto you. Love never fails. I have you in the palm of My hand; and none such can pluck you out. Your Ever-encompassing Father God.

War Cry ("War" then "Peace") Part Two
by God

The world will pass away; but you and My Words (the Bible) live on and on and on for eternity.

Life in the Vine - entwined forever more. This is what I want My people, My church, to ponder on. Eye hath not seen nor ear heard what your Father God has in store for you. Will I not do it? Will it not come to pass? Hath not My Word been fulfilled since the beginning of time? Did I not say I know each hair on your head and every sparrow that falls? Then why fret over the future when all is in My Hands?

Love Me and know that out of the body, present with the Lord; and in the body, present with the Lord. Your Ever-lasting God.

"My passion..."

My Passion
by God

Beloved, My Passion is beyond measure for mankind. You and all like you are to Me, My food and drink (My substance). It is to love and be loved in return. My Passion is for you; and yours, for Me. This was the epitome of My Son's existence, His love for Me passed out for you. It is the strongest emotion of love that has ever existed. It is a passion willing to give one's life for another — His for yours.

Do you have this much passion for Him My child?

Do you remember when Christ asked Peter three times if he loved Him? Did he really love Him enough to give his life? Peter answered, "Yes! Yes! Yes!" - three times. Jesus told Him what would come about for him. Peter, therefore, was informed and prepared. Are you?

Many today have this passion for Me and love their life not unto death. Little one, I know this is serious; but then you live in awesome days. I AM holding you in the palm of My Hand. My Banner over you is Love, Love, Love. Your Passionate Abba Father. (Psalm 91)

"*Do you have this much passion for Him...*"

"It is a passion willing to give one's life for another — His for yours."

Truth (What is Truth?)
by God

John 16:13 "Howbeit when he, the Spirit of truth, is come, he will guide you into all truth: for he shall not speak of himself, but whatsoever he shall hear, that shall he speak: and he will show you things to come."

Today, as always, one asks, "What is truth?" Did not Pontius Pilate ask this same question of Jesus? Can you answer this question?

"I am the Way, the Truth, and the Life: no man cometh unto the Father, but by Me." (John 14:6)

In My Word, the Bible, the secrets to all Truth are revealed one after the other after the other and after the other. My Words are true. I AM cannot lie. Believe them and live. Deny them and die in your falsehoods.

Satan is the father of all lies. There is a spirit of lying that can enter man; and he will choose to lie when the Truth is before him. Choose not to open yourself to that Spirit of falsehood. Choose Truth every time and escape that spirit's entrance. What a happy life you will lead. Just ask Me for help when difficultly comes. My Spirit of Truth and Wisdom can lead you to all Truth. Ask Me for the Spirit of Wisdom to lead you into all Truth. My Holy Spirit searches the deep things of life and can reveal them unto you. Just ask Him. He is with you and in you. Then ask for My Gift of Love and Wisdom to help you and explain all Truth. I love My Children and want them to know My Truth and then be truthful.

Your Loving And Truthful Abba Father.

"My stamp is on your forehead. It is the sign of the cross..."

IDENTITY (THE UNITY OF THE HUMAN AND DIVINE)
by God

"Ye are Mine," sayeth the Lord. I made man for My Pleasure and made it possible for him to identify with Me and for Me to identify with My creature. Remember, in Genesis, We said, "Let us make man in Our Image." My Son breathed on this piece of lifeless clay; and man became a living soul. God breathed. And My heart's desire is for every man who has breath to praise the Lord.

Can you believe that this can be and will be because of your identity with Me? I AM grooming you for eternity. All of you are stamped in the palm of My Hand (like cattle) to identify that you are mine. Also, My stamp is on your forehead. It is the sign of the cross; because your identity is protected with blood and paid for in advance.

You, My Children, are One in Your Father God. We are identified by My Son's death, burial, and resurrection. Your soul and spirit are linked to ours. You are our identity; and we are yours. We match. Our Blood Line is at Pentecost. You are tagged with Your Father's identity now and forever more. Your Creator and Identifier, Jehovah.

A song, *"You are my everything; you are my all. You are my everything, both great and small."*

God's response: "I AM your everything. I AM your all. I AM your everything, both great and small."

Light

by God

I AM the Light of the world. In Me, there is no darkness. Yes, My child, who can explain My Light? 'Tis a mystery, isn't it?

"Yes, Lord, I love the light — the natural and the spiritual. I love for You to show Light on scripture. I love when the morning comes and Your Light penetrates my window. It's like a new birth each morning in the day that is dawning. I love the sun rays coming through my bevel edged windows, reflecting rainbow colors all over my dressing room and into my bedroom. Now, Father (Abba), tell Me what You love about Light."

Yes, My child, My Light can penetrate the darkness. Darkness cannot destroy My Light. My Light can shine through clay vessels of My Creation and radiate My Love, My Power, My Anointing, My Truth. My Light is elegant and soft and can be powerful and destroying. My Light can give life or also destroy life. My Light is necessary for all life to exist. In the beginning, the earth was null and void.

And I said, "Let there be light." And there was light; and I saw that it was good! Where I AM, there is light. And where I AM not, there is darkness. Did I not say in My Word, when I give My Light into a vessel (human), don't hide it under a table; but let it shine for all to see and be drawn to Me by that Divine Light?

Look at Moses' face after he was in My Presence for forty days. Your face, too, can shine like Moses' after You have encountered My Presence (My Glory).

A song, *"I desire for you to be My Sunbeam and shine for Me each day. A Sunbeam. Just be a Sunbeam for Me."*

I love each of you with My Lightning Rods, My connection from Me to you. From The Father Of Lights, Your Creator.

PREDESTINATION
by God

Oh my! What a question you do ask of Me, my little one. Remember, I AM God, your Maker. So why do you ask the potter who is and who is not My Chosen - which ones are cracked and thrown away and which ones are whole and contain My Water (the Holy Spirit)? I AM the potter, and you are the clay; so why ask Me which ones are thrown away?

I AM God; and there is none other. Many are called; but few are chosen. The question is though I have chosen you all, why some will not choose Me. I know who will and who will not. Let's go back to the wheat and the tares. Remember, I said they are left alone until the harvest; and I tell My angels which ones to pick and which ones to leave. My Holy Spirit has made many ripe for plucking right now; but where are My earthly harvesters? Pray that I send laborers into the harvest.

But now to get back to your question. Yes, I AM a merciful God and have shared much mercy on some and little on some. How I love to see the wretched have a change of heart. They need much more mercy than others.

Yes, My Child, your God is all knowing, infinite. You are all finite and will never know all things. I AM and can do as I please about anything and everything. Just know that I have chosen you; and all is well with your soul. Leave it there at the foot of the cross. Your Loving Merciful Father and God Jehovah.

A song, *"At the Cross, at the Cross, where I first saw the light; and now I am happy all the day."*

Another song, *"There is no secret what God can do - and what he's done for others, he'll do for you. With arms wide open, he'll pour it on you. There is no secret what God can do."*

Another song, *"Thank you Lord for saving my soul. Thank you Lord for making me whole.*

"Creator of Wonders."

WONDER
by God

Ah, sweet mystery of Life. My wonder is your wonderment. Holy wonder is the splendor in your life. Your words cannot explain My wonderment. No words can explain Me. I AM that I AM. My wonder is like the wind. You know when it comes. You are aware of its fulfillment; but you did not conceive it or plan it or make it possible, nor can you control it. You can only watch it unfold and standby and be amazed by the wonderment of it all.

In the Kingdom of God, there is a wonder a minute. Most go unnoticed by the eye. But the eye of My spiritual beings see them and recognize the splendor of My wonders and give Me Glory. I have many wonders the world has not seen. Some of my wonders include: (a) the stars in heaven (b) the moon at night (c) the sun in the morning (d) the winter snow (e) beautiful sunrises (f) the green grass (g) the wild flowers (h) all My species of trees (i) a new born baby (j) the Immaculate Birth of My Son (k) the sunset on different evenings (l) the human body (man) (m) all animals (n) water (o) the human mind (p) angels (q) birds singing and talking. All of these are confirmed in Job and Psalms.

To My born ones, I AM their wonderful Father God. In that statement is a big mystery to all others (a sweet mystery of life; to them a mystery, to us a wonderment). To me, Christmas is my wonderment. Your Creator of Wonders.

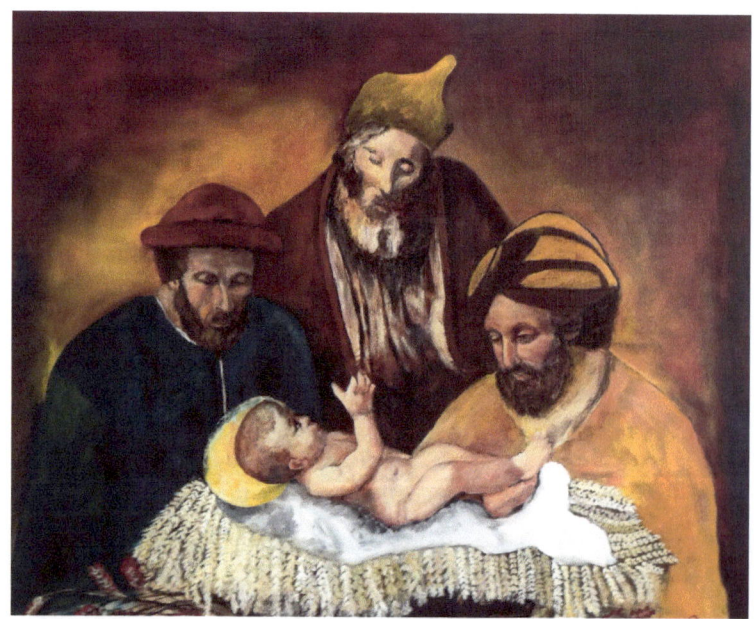

"...to us a wonderment."

"...be amazed by the wonderment of it all."

BEHOLD
by God

Stop, look, and listen. A wonder is about to happen. Your God is ready to move on your behalf.

Watch Him manifest Himself for all to see. He is ready to show Himself to all mankind. Many will recognize Him and turn and repent and make themselves ready for His coming. Now is the time, My people, to dress yourself with My fine linen of purity. Remove the spots and blemishes. I AM coming for people without spots or blemishes.

Oh Lord, please show us how to do all this.

Make Me your object of affection. Make Me the object of your confession. Let Me be your knight in shining armor. Let Me be your king of kings. Let Me be your lover of your soul. Let Me be your one and only God. I could go on and on; but St. Paul said it all - know Me in the power of resurrection and conformity of death. "For to me, to live is Christ, and to die is gain" (Phil. 1:21). (Oh my Lord, you are so magnificent.) Your Beholding Father.

A song, *"Lord, I just want to love you, love you with all my heart. And Lord, I just want to bless you. Lord, I just want to caress you."*

A song, *"Thank you Lord for saving my soul. Thank you Lord for making me whole."*

Janie Allen

"...make Me your object of affection, make Me the object of your confession."

"I Am coming..."

ADOLESCENCE
by God

You ask the question, 'Why Lord? Why Lord did you make a time in our growth called adolescence or teens? Could we not have just skipped over that stage in our life span?' Well, let Me tell you why. Did the clay ask the potter, 'Why did you make me like this?' I AM that I AM; and I made man to withstand all periods of his mortal life span. Think back a few years of your own life. You needed each decade before you could go forward to the next. You could not have advanced from 10 to 20 without going through your teens.

I AM the Creator and a Mastermind. Many processes take place during those years that you cannot see. Hormones, glands, bones all are in movement and fall in place. At this time, one's own body is in constant motion. Am I not able to bring these loved ones through? Satan has set a trap for them; but with the prayers of My Saints, they can and do come through.

There is a time and season for all stages of life. Each one has its rewards. My plan is for teenagers to be a delightful memory for both them and their parents. Satan's plan is for them to be unruly, rebellious, sarcastic, unduly wild, and to overdose. Remember, he comes to rob and steal and even kill. I tell you that unless I come quickly, the next generation of teenagers will not survive. This generation barely did.

The fields are white for harvesting for the harvesters. Pray that they hunger and thirst after righteousness. Pray that I will assign angels for them and their teachers (angelic protection). Pray that they receive the gifts of My Holy Spirit (discernment of spirit). Pray that I send them Christian counselors. Pray that I send people with unconditional agape love to counsel them into maturity. Pray for their parents to have My divine understanding and wisdom to guide and cherish them. Pray that they do not harbor guilt and unforgiveness. Pray that drugs and drink (alcohol) will be distasteful to them. Pray that they seek My face and turn to Me for deliverance. Pray for patience for their parents. Pray for their salvation!! Pray for Christians to pray. Pray for their teachers, counselors, and churches to seek God for guidance to see them through to maturity. Pray for My love to shine through you, for them to see Me; for I love them oh so tenderly.

HOPE AND PEACE
by God

"These things I have spoken unto you, that in me ye might have peace. In the world ye shall have tribulation: but be of good cheer; I have overcome the world." (John 16:33) Fear not My children. You are in Me. I have overcome the world; and you can too. I in you-you, Me, and We are in the Father. Yours and Mine - beloved, this is the hope of all mankind. Can you see this? In fact, this is one's only hope at this time of your existence on planet earth. The signs I tell you about in Matthew 24 are taking place in all parts of your universe day and night. Your hope now comes from Me, your Redeemer, and Our Father Jehovah.

Song, *"On solid rock I stand; on Jesus Christ and righteousness."*

"Now faith is the substance of things hoped for, the evidence of things not seen." (Heb. 11) Yes, My little ones, will I find faith when I return? At this time on your time clock you can understand this saying of mine. "Oh no", you are saying, "Oh Lord, what must we do?" I say, "Stand. The battle is mine, your faith and hope in Me will carry you through. Oh yes, take heed to occupy till I come. Fulfill your place in My Kingdom."

Song, *"Trust and obey for there is no other way but to trust and obey."*

Faithful and True, Jesus.

Song, *"On solid rock I stand, all else is sinking sand."*

Song, *"My hope is built on nothing else but Jesus Christ and righteousness."*

Vanity (Vain)
by God

My children, vanity is a deceitful force. Once it takes root, it is hard to uproot. Being vain is spoken of by the world as unmerited pride (pride in one's self; pride in one's possessions; pride in one's own flesh; pride in one's accomplishments, knowledge, wisdom, ability, skills). Can you not see that none of these are lasting unless I am involved? I give; and I take away. I wound; and I kill; and I make alive. All is vanity unless My Holy Spirit is there. If I remove My Spirit, all is lost. Satan comes and fills the void.

As Solomon said, "Vexation of Spirit." Read what Solomon wrote about vanity in Ecclesiastes (Chapter 1). Vanity destroys a Christian's witness. Vanity destroys and eats at one's soul and spirit. Vanity can become "idolic" and can replace Me in your life. Put Me first, and vanity flees. Put Me second, and vanity creeps in. Put Me third, and peace is erased. Put Me fourth, and I AM no longer at all. You are as a walking dead man.

So My little ones, flee from the sin of being vain. "How?" you say. Flee from this sin by rehearsing My ten commandments daily and by reading My Word daily. Prayer at the end of each day puts that day at the foot of the cross. "To live is for Christ and to die is gain." Vanity is being vain. I, your God and Father, can make and break. (Ecc 3:14)

Song, *"Oh how he loves you and me. Oh how he loves you and me. He sent his son. His will be done. Oh how he loves you and me."*

My love for you, and yours for Me can do this.

The Kingdom of God
by God

One sweet mystery of Life — many are called; but few are chosen. Which one are you? For it is your choice, My child. I chose you, but the question is, "Do you choose Me?" Can and have you left all for Me and My Kingdom? Or do you still cling on to some of your past idols (anything that comes between you and Me)? I have to, and need to, be first. You see, I know you as no one else; and I know what is best for you. Also, what I have for you is above all else no matter can replace divinity. All else is rubbish compared to My Kingdom, Love, and My Gifts.

The Kingdom of God is neither meat nor drink but Love, Joy, and Peace in the Holy Spirit. Also, My Holy Spirit will give you Our power (dynamite) to conquer all inequity if you will let Him. Sometimes it is a matter of life and death. (The violent take it by force.) Now My loved ones, the Kingdom (My Kingdom) is within — not without. Soon and very soon it will be apparent. But now I AM removing all rubbish from you and replacing it with Love, Joy, Peace, Long Suffering, Gentleness, Kindness — preparing you to reign throughout eternity.

Remember the ten virgins. Some had not removed enough rubbish and needed more time. "Too late." Stop, look, and listen. Now is the time to make your slate clean. You are not alone in your situation. Call on your mate (Holy Spirit) to keep you. He is at your side, ready to abide, ready to give all His gifts for Christ Jesus' bride. (Remember Rebekah and Isaac.)

Oh how He has so much gold and silver for you to reside in My Kingdom forever and ever. All He wants is all of you. Please make room for Him. Recognize His duties. My Son has given Him to make you holy as He is holy. My Son is deserving of a virgin bride dressed in pure white linen. He is willing to redress you. Please My little ones let him. Today is the day of your rehearsal dinner; for tomorrow is your wedding day.

Song: *"There is a river that comes from deep within. There is a river that cleanses from sin."*

Song: *"Holy Spirit, you are welcome in my place. Holy Spirit, you are welcome in my place."*

Coming Again
by God

A song: *"Coming again, coming again - may be morning, may be noon, may be evening...may be soon."*

I AM coming again. (Rev. 14)

Behold, I stand at your door and knock (Rev. 3:20). Yes, I have come spiritually; and now, physically. Yes, have you opened your door and let Me come in to sup with you? For you who have made yourselves ready for your departure with Me (not spiritually, but physically), continue to sup with Me each and every day until this happens. Your manna will come daily, just like it came for the Israelites in their wilderness.

Now, My called out ones, your directions will come only from Me, your lifegiver. Only I, can sustain your life at this moment in your time span. I AM your way, your truth, and your very life. I AM your vine, just like your mother's umbilical cord when you were in her womb. Without this food you will die and wither away. I AM the vine; and you are the branches. Without Me, you are nothing and can do nothing. Abide in Me; and your strength and nourishment will always come. My Father and yours was in everything from the beginning. His Will (divine will) shall be fulfilled. You are a piece of the puzzle in His beautiful masterpiece. Can you behold all of this? Oh what a beautiful painting, when all pieces are finally in place. Oh what a wonderful day it will be, when I see you face to face. Your Alpha and Omega. Your Father, Son, and Holy Spirit.

Our Father (Father's Day) Part One
by God

Our Father which art in heaven,
Hallowed be Thy Name.
Thy kingdom come.
Thy will be done
in earth, as it is in heaven.

I AM your Father God - your Alpha and Omega.

As Abraham was, I AM. I AM a family man. I married Israel and produced by My Holy Spirit, a Son, who inherited My characteristics (Trinity). He was the first fruit of My womb, but paved the way for many more sons and daughters by the same Holy Spirit. (Born of the Spirit, born from above, born of the Spirit, out of My love.) Your family on earth is patterned from My Family.

A song: *"This is my story, this is my song. Loving my family all the day long."*

Your loving Father and Holy God.

Janie Allen

OUR FATHER (FATHER'S DAY) PART TWO
by God

And why did I need a family (procreation)? Mainly, I desire to be loved and to love in return, to be praised and worshiped, to share My innermost things with My children, to give to them of Me (gifts of My Spirit) - all the things you do with your father and children. The gift of My love through My Son is the greatest gift for all mankind. The force of My love is indefinable, indescribable, unconditional, and forgiving of all your mistakes. All of these can also be yours for your family. Your heavenly Father is a family man with a plan. My Son and His bride will always abide and provide. Your Creator and Father God.

WAR & PEACE
by God

My peace I give and leave with you. Not as the world gives you; for in Me only, will one find peace. In the world is tribulation and war. Through Me only, is there perfect peace. I AM in you; and you are in Me. We are attached to our Father God. Therefore, I have overcome the World Wars and you can too.

That sounds so good and easy; but it is so very hard for us to achieve.

That is exactly why I went back to the Father to give you My Holy Spirit. Rom 8:16 "The Spirit itself beareth witness with our spirit, that we are children of God..."

The Holy Spirit is your enabler to see you through to perfect peace and perfection. I (Jesus) achieved this; and so can you. War is inevitable - outside you and inside you. Scripture tells us why they cry out Peace, Peace, Peace and there is no Peace. All the world is crying for Peace. All everyone wants is Peace within and without. But I tell you this cannot be without Me and My Holy Spirit. (John 14:27) "Peace I leave with you, my peace I give unto you: not as the world giveth, give I unto you. Let not your heart be troubled, neither let it be afraid." Only with Me and in Me is perfect peace. My soon coming will end War from without and within. Look up. Your redemption is so very close. War and destruction is all around. But you can be in the eye of this hurricane (storm, tornados). For in the eye of the storm is peace and quietness. Your Prince of Peace, Jesus Christ.

Janie Allen

The Brain (Computer and Human)
by God

The brain is compared to a spoke in a wheel. It holds the whole body together. Many, many neutrons are the electricity that sparks the brain machine into action. Your brain has many parts. All have their own function. Man's finite mind cannot understand or comprehend the infinite mind. The brain is the master control of your body. Only your Creator designed it. It is similar to mine. Selah.

Man is made in My image. (Gen. 1 & 2) Because man is made in My image, he can think somewhat like Me. Yes, he is trying to figure Me and My creation out (literally picking it to pieces), even cloning or creating human life. This My child will never be done successfully; because I AM God and there is no other.

Man is wonderfully and fearfully made. (Ps 139:14) I will put an end to this endeavor. Their cloning will not be in My image. I will mar all their endeavors. Can you see why? Unregenerate man is evil; and no good can come from his hand. I wound; and I heal. I kill; and I make alive. Your God is an Awesome God. You, creature, are an awesome creation. Like Father like Son.

My plan for man will not now or ever be destroyed. Man's plan to make man will disintegrate into the dust of what man began. Only My Holy Spirit can understand the mechanisms of all the components of man inside and out. The brain is a complex organism not to be tampered with. The only power that can change the mechanical structure of man's brain is by prayer and the Holy Spirit. The best man can do is try.

Any Christian can have more power by prayer than a surgeon can with a knife. Prayer is the mediator between life and death. I know My little one that you do not fully understand all this about Me; because you are finite, and I AM infinite. Now shut your eyes and go to sleep. Your Divine Creator, Alpha and Omega.

P.S.. I love all of you so much. My hand is not shortened that it cannot always save and heal.

"Man is wonderfully and fearfully made."

WHAT IS TRUTH?
by God

"...I AM the way, the truth, and the life: no man cometh unto the Father, but by Me." (John 14:6)

It is so simple - My Word, your Bible, is the truth all are searching and looking for from the beginning of time. My child, did I not put that question in you so you would search for Me with all your heart, soul, and mind? Satan has blinded so many lives. Please pray that eyes and ears be opened to hunger and thirst for truth and righteousness; or just to know Me as their Creator and My Son Jesus Christ for their Savior.

Anyone who seeks Me with all their heart and mind, I will reveal Myself to them. Then if they will confess Me to themselves and each other, I will come and make My abode with them as long as I am allowed too. I will fill them with My love for Me and for each other. I will give them My Holy Spirit to know Me better and My ways in all things; to know the truth - right from wrong. I will hear them if they ask for more of My Spirit to give them power to overcome their enemy (satan). My Holy Spirit will teach and guide them to all My truths. Jesus Christ is My only begotten Son - yesterday, today, and forever. Selah, Your Father and Holy God.

Jesus, you are a great big and wonderful God; and I love you so very much.

Song: *"Jesus loves us this we know, for the Bible tells us so..."*

Song: *"Jesus paid it all..."*

"Life, Death, Resurrection."

Life, Death, Resurrection
by God

This is the crux to eternity. It is pictured all around you. It is LIFE! You exist and were born for this metamorphosis of life, death, and resurrection. My plan. Can you say, to live is for Christ and to die is gain, as Saint Paul did? This is the answer to life. As for you, the pattern of life is Jesus Christ. He is the Way, the Truth, and the Life; and no one can come to Me except through Him.

For you, the sting of death has been removed. You passed from death unto life in a twinkling of an eye - from one dimension to another. I birthed you to live with Me for eternity. Death came from disobedience. In Adam, all died. In Christ, all are made alive. I have redeemed you from a life of destruction and crowned you with loving kindness and tender mercies. Psalm 103

My children, you are all resurrected in My book; so do not fear death as the heathens do. I desire all My children to say as My Son did, I did not come to be ministered to but to minister and give My life a ransom for many. Many of His disciples did just that and are still doing that today.

Song: *"Because He lives, you can face tomorrow. Just and only because He lives."*

Song: *"This is your story; this is your song. Loving your Savior all the day long."*

This is worth singing for. This is why I made song. Listen to My Creation. They are constantly singing to Me. Please! Please! Let the Holy Spirit sing His song through you. We are so in tune to His tune.

Song: *"In my heart, there rings a melody, rings a melody to Heaven's harmony. In my heart there rings a melody, rings a melody to Heaven's harmony."*

Can you see now that life, death, and resurrection is just a pattern for your wedding attire on your wedding day? You see, My child, it is really very simple; but My children make life so complicated.

You can do all things in your life through Jesus Christ who strengthens you. I AM THE ALPHA AND THE OMEGA.

Song: *"Holy, Holy, Holy! Lord God Almighty"*.

In the Kingdom of God, there are no winters.

Fear

by God

I have not given you a spirit of fear but of love, power, and a sound mind. My children, did I not say to all of you: fear not at all times then and now? My hand is on you at all times - in the body or out. In My Word I say; when you walk through the waters, even the fires, I AM with you. My Spirit is within you. Just call on Me and activate Him on your behalf.

Oh My children! Can't you feel My love for you; caressing you, guiding you, protecting you?

Remember, I said to My family the Israelites, "How I would love to gather you under My wings as a mother hen her chicks." But she would not let Me. I say the same to You. So will you let Me? Under My protection there is warmth and safety from all harm. I have provided a place for you whether in the body or not. My arms can always hold you. Did I not rescue Peter when he started to fear and go under the water? Just call My name - Jesus - your Savior, for I AM your survival kit. Father, Son, and Holy Spirit; yesterday, today, and forever - Your Alpha and Omega.

P.S. My love is overwhelming.

Song: *"What the world needs now is love, love, love..."*

"*...Your Alpha and Omega.*"

Resolve and Resolutions Mine and Yours
by God

Mine — I came; I conquered; and I returned! Now My little one, what is yours?

Almost the same. I came because of you, Jesus.

I can conquer. And I shall return. Now for the in-betweens. My Father gave you a free will to choose soon after birth. Your resolutions depend on you. My Father has given you the standards (Ten Commandments); but you have the free will to refuse or commit to them. Because of My resolve then (the cross) and now, you fortunately have the ability or power to achieve them. Do you understand this beloved? My resolve for you is for you and My church to resolve to do My Father's will. All of My newsletters (Kingdom of God Newspaper Headlines) that have been given to you in the past two years are for you to distribute to all I bring forth to you. To whom much is given, much is required. I love you and love our contact with each other. You are My creation; and I AM the Creator. I long to commune with My creation. Behold, what an amazing day it will be when this will be made possible as in the Garden with Adam and Eve (1st man and woman). Remember, I walked and talked with them; and we discussed the day that was and the day that is and the day that will be.

Song: *"I come to the garden alone. And He walks with me and talks with me and tells me I am His own."*

P.S. Father, you are truly who you say you are — our Daddy, our PaPa God. Lord, you are truly who you say you are — the lover of our souls.

Song: *"I love you truly."* (Wedding Song) Bride and Groom are coming down the aisle.

"God's Kingdom News" is an inspiring book that shares His wondrous power and His wondrous love. After reading this treasure your life will never be the same. The artist is the author's gifted daughter. Very rarely have I been given the privilege of sharing about something so exquisite.

Carole S. Garland
Precept Bible Study Leader and devoted friend

Your paintings have brought an old world feeling to these words of God through our beloved Janie. It is as if she was some ancient mystic whose words are traveling forward to our present time and past us into the future. I loved how you extracted a phrase of text and really emphasized it by placing it below an appropriate painting. Your rendering of Mary was very moving as she bore her family upon her back. I was thrilled with your different renderings of Jesus. To me it underscores the fact that He is all things to all people and all can identify with Him as He has so identified Himself with each one of us. You have enhanced and magnified these living messages of our dear Janie and her amazing relationship of devoted love for our Lord.

Claudia Cardwell

God's Kingdom News
available on Amazon.com

Prints of the original paintings are available at
DianneGuthrieFineArt.com
or by contacting Dianne at
dianne.guthrie@hotmail.com

www.ingramcontent.com/pod-product-compliance
Lightning Source LLC
Chambersburg PA
CBHW041544220426
43665CB00002B/26